HAUNTED TUSCALOOSA

DAVID HIGDON AND BRETT J. TALLEY

Haunted America

Published by Haunted America
A Division of The History Press
Charleston, SC 29403
www.historypress.net

Images are courtesy of the authors unless otherwise noted.

First published 2012

Manufactured in the United States

ISBN 978.1.60949.573.2

Library of Congress CIP data applied for.

This book is dedicated to Marvin Lee Harper,

1919–2009,

the "Dean and Patron" of heritage preservation in West Alabama.

CONTENTS

CONTENTS

ACKNOWLEDGEMENTS

The authors would like to thank the innumerable people who helped to make this book possible, from the people who agreed to share their stories to the friends and family members who supported us throughout the process of writing the book. We couldn't have done it without you, and this book is truly as much a testament to you as it is to us.

Still, some people deserve special recognition. David would like to thank his wife, Debbie, who has stood beside him through good times and bad, and his four children, who have inspired him to pursue this project.

As for Brett, he would like his parents, Mike and Sue Talley, to know that this book is for them. They inspired his love of history and his desire to always seek the truth. He would be nothing without them, and this book is but one part of his life that he was able to accomplish only because of their love.

Finally, Brett would also like to dedicate this book to his nephew, Cristian. Read, learn and remember.

INTRODUCTION

The city of Tuscaloosa and the University of Alabama are more than just dots on a map. History clings to them, as do myth and legend. They sit on land that has seen the ancient native tribes come and go. The land was there when the first settlers came, and on it was built a city that is quintessentially southern. The great planters of the antebellum age built homes there, and they watched their city burn in the fires of the Civil War. From those ashes came the University of Alabama, the heart of the state's intellectual life and home to what would become a national sports power. Some of the greatest battles of the civil rights era were won there, and today the city and the university are taking the state into the twenty-first century and beyond. That's the official history, but there is so much more to a town and a school than that.

It is off the pages of your normal history book where myth, legend and history collide. And that is where the truth becomes murky. In this book, you will hear the stories of Tuscaloosa and the University of Alabama that don't always make it into the histories. Some of them are twice-told tales, passed down from one family to another, told by grandmothers and grandfathers to their grandkids just as their parents' parents told them. Others come from eyewitnesses, things that they saw or heard firsthand and could not explain—at least by any normal, rational explanation.

In the pages of this book, you will hear tales of haunted houses and shadows moving through university buildings. We will enter abandoned insane asylums, antebellum homes and ancient cemeteries. We will review stories of long-dead Civil War soldiers, of women driven insane by the death of lovers and of some leading lights of Tuscaloosa who still walk in the massive homes they constructed. In this book, there are children who died too early, professors who never left the classroom and even the spirit of a collie that still serves its master, long after his death.

Some will criticize these stories, saying that they are not real history. But that raises a question. What is *real* history? Sure, we know the dates and the major players, but the color, the heart of the matter—*that* we see through the eyewitness. We know what it was like when Washington crossed the Delaware, when Lincoln gave the Gettysburg Address or when the first news of the bombing of Pearl Harbor started spreading across the country because of the words and experiences of ordinary people.

That is what you will hear within these pages. You will see the history of Tuscaloosa and the University of Alabama, but you will also see the shadows of that history. The things left behind. They are part of that history, too. And if the people you will meet within these pages are to be believed, some of that history is still with us, even to this day. You just have to know where to look and not be afraid to hear the voices of those long gone and long dead.

PART I
THE STORIES OF TUSCALOOSA

In the central part of Alabama, in the last foothills of the Appalachian Mountain chain, on the banks of the mighty Black Warrior River, sits the fifth-largest city in Alabama—a place called Tuscaloosa. While the city as we now know it was founded in 1819, the roots of Tuscaloosa go back much further than that to the darkest pre-history of the region.

Just south of the city of Tuscaloosa sits an archaeological site known as Moundville, one that represents the ancient American Indian roots of the area. Designated as a National Historic Landmark, Moundville is the second-largest site of an ancient Native American society that is known as Middle Mississippian, a culture that stretched from Illinois to the central Mississippi River Valley. The site is named for the large platform mounds that rise throughout what was once a walled American Indian city. The mounds resemble flattop pyramids of dirt, the largest rising some sixty feet. At its height, the city contained over ten thousand people, but the site is shrouded in utter mystery. Why the people came there, why they built the great earthen mounds and why they eventually abandoned the site in what appears to have been a great rush is completely unknown. The artifacts uncovered there, while enigmatic, are not helpful in deciphering what disaster befell Moundville's inhabitants. All we know for certain is that by AD 1500, the site had been abandoned.

The other native tribes that surrounded Moundville remained, however, and when explorer and conquistador Hernando de Soto came to claim the southeastern United States for the Spanish, he found them waiting for his expedition. They weren't happy to see him, either.

De Soto had made a name for himself in the mountainous land of the Incan Empire, riding at the side of famed conquistador Francisco Pizarro during his conquest of South America. De Soto had led one of the groups of Spanish cavalry that captured Atahualpa, emperor of the Incas. He had accomplished this remarkable feat despite being outnumbered, 80,000 Incan troops to 180 Spaniards. De Soto's audacity and willingness to take insane challenges for the glory of king and Crown—and his own pockets—impressed his commanders back in Europe. They quickly gave him command of his own expedition, and De Soto returned to the New World with 620 men and 220 horses. He landed on the shores of what is now known as the state of Florida in 1539. What started out as a glorious expedition would end with his death by fever in 1542. But it is what happened in between that interests us the most.

De Soto left an indelible mark on the South. During his travels, De Soto came upon a tribe of American Indians known to us as the Muskogeans. The leader of that tribe was called by the name Tuskaloosa. Chief Tuskaloosa was the kind of man who was born to make an impact. Standing a full foot and a half taller than the largest of the Spanish soldiers, Chief Tuskaloosa was as wise in the way he handled the Spaniards as he was tall of stature.

Whether he had heard tales of their conquests or simply had some uncanny sixth sense, the chief immediately marked the Spaniards as a threat. When De Soto arrived in Atahachi, the chief's home and the capital of the Muskogean nation, Chief Tuskaloosa knew that he did not have a large enough army to defeat the well-armed and well-equipped Spanish troops. De Soto, accustomed to getting whatever he wanted, made demands on Tuskaloosa that the chief turn over native women to his soldiers. Tuskaloosa promised De Soto that while he would relent, the Spanish would need to travel to the town of Mabila to acquire the women they sought. Tuskaloosa allowed De Soto to take him hostage as security on that promise.

De Soto found Mabila in a region of central Alabama near present-day Tuscaloosa. The Spaniards found a fortress town, one enclosed in thick walls made from bound tree trunks and dried mud. The Spanish had been promised women, and they knew something was amiss when they noticed that the town was populated almost exclusively by young male warriors. In fact, Mabila was a Trojan horse. When the Spanish arrived, they were beset by hundreds of native warriors.

De Soto barely escaped with his life. When the Battle of Mabila had ended, 200 Spaniards were dead and 150 severely wounded, while 3,000

Indians were killed. Chief Tuskaloosa was one of the dead. The Spanish burned Mabila to the ground.

The Spanish did not celebrate their victory. With half their men dead or wounded, their supplies destroyed and many of their horses lost, the Spanish fled into the wilderness. They were pursued by enemies on every side. De Soto found himself harassed throughout the rest of his campaign, eventually dying and being buried in the middle of the Mississippi River to prevent natives from finding his grave and desecrating his body. The legend of Tuskaloosa lived on, however, and the chief would become immortal when the founders of Tuscaloosa named their city after him.

Tuscaloosa's central location and easy river access made it one of early Alabama's most critical towns. In 1826, the capital of Alabama came to the city, and the University of Alabama was established there in 1831. When the capital moved to Montgomery in 1846, Tuscaloosa's fortunes took a hit, though the establishment of the Bryce State Hospital for the Insane helped to mollify the loss of prestige.

Local planters and businessmen made fortunes during that period, and great antebellum mansions rose throughout Tuscaloosa and its sister city of Northport. There's no telling the grandeur Tuscaloosa might have reached, but the middle of the nineteenth century brought a devastating civil war that would impoverish the defeated South and its people for at least the next one hundred years. By 1865, the Confederacy had been vanquished, and Union troops had burned the University of Alabama, a military college during the war, to the ground.

But as the Black Warrior River had built Tuscaloosa, so too would it rebuild it. In the 1890s, a series of locks and dams were constructed along the river, opening up a water route all the way to the port city of Mobile on the Alabama coast of the Gulf of Mexico. The coal mines and steel mills in the area boomed as a result, and people once again flocked to Tuscaloosa.

The city has continued to grow and is now the center of a burgeoning automotive industry in the state, with Mercedes Benz building its first automotive assembly plant in North America just outside the city in 1993. Tuscaloosa is a modern city with centuries of history. And woven throughout that history are legends, folklore and stories of things that walk in the shadows, not all of which can be explained. Below we chronicle some of their stories, and together we will seek to discover the truth of the spirits and specters that are said to haunt the halls of the city of Tuscaloosa.

THE DRISH MANSION

In 1941, Walker Evans would publish what is now widely regarded as one of the finest works of photojournalism: *Let Us Now Praise Famous Men*. Within its pages, Evans revealed to a recovering world the ravages of the Great Depression with a clarity and immediacy that mere words could not express. The book went on to be something of a cultural phenomenon and has had an impact on journalism and the study of history to this day.

That is the story that most people know. But there is another story, one far older, behind one of Evans's most famous images: "The Tuscaloosa Wrecking Company."

Evans took the picture while on his travels through the South, collecting the history of a region that had once flourished but had been devastated by the aftermath of the Civil War, hardly having recovered by the time of the Great Depression. We can't know what Evans thought when he snapped the image, but we can imagine. Here was what had been a magnificent plantation home, a white-pillared southern Colonial masterpiece dedicated to the wealth of the region. Now it was a symbol of the Depression, with its once beautiful windows broken out and boarded up and its opulence dedicated to car repair. Evans probably took the picture and moved on to the next town and the next sad story, never knowing the true tragedy that haunted the halls of what is known today as the Drish Mansion.

In the early 1800s, the Owen brothers moved with their fortune, slaves and widowed sister to a frontier town in the new territory of Alabama. The locals called the little village Tuskaloosa, named after a legendary Indian chief killed by Hernando De Soto some three hundred years earlier. While De Soto won the battle, he lost the war, and the five tribes of Creeks, Chickasaws, Choctaws, Chippewas and Cherokees dominated the state for a couple hundred years more. That is, until Andrew Jackson brought his army to the state, intent on opening it to colonization by eastern whites hungry for more land. His decisive victory at the Battle of Horseshoe Bend quickly made that possible. Now cleared of hostile natives, Alabama was opened to settlement, and the Owens joined a flood of eastern settlers seeking new and unspoiled land to cultivate.

The Owens were quite wealthy, and their sister, the widow Sarah McKinney, was considered something of a catch by the many enterprising young men of the region. She quickly caught the eye of Dr. John Drish, a skilled physician in town and a man of moderate means. Dr. Drish was not only charming, but he was smart and ambitious too. He was well aware that

The Drish Mansion.

a wife's fortune passed to her husband upon marriage, and he had every intention of rising in the world using Sarah's wealth. After considerable effort, Drish won the hand of McKinney, and she joined Dr. Drish and his daughter, Katherine (from an earlier marriage), on his farm.

Perhaps they would have been happy there, living out their lives in relative obscurity. But Dr. Drish had several vices, one of which was his jealousy and competition with Robert Jemison Jr., another wealthy planter in town. When Jemison announced his plans to build a magnificent mansion less than half a mile away, Drish started to draw up his own plans to turn his simple brick home into a plantation house that could compete with the best Jemison had to offer. Galleries were added on either side of the original structure, with Ionic and Doric columns to decorate them. A tower was built in the center from which it was said Dr. Drish could observe the construction of the Jemison home and plan to better it. Perhaps it was because the Drish Mansion rose on the back of jealousy and hate that tragedy would come to haunt its halls for most of its history.

It began with his daughter, Katherine. Katherine was said to be a beautiful girl and quite prized by the gentlemen of Tuscaloosa County.

Despite the best efforts of Dr. Drish, however, her father could find no young man who would meet her high standards. To make matters worse, Drish was insistent that any match be one of the wealth and high breeding he had come to expect in his own life. It started to look as if Katherine might never find a husband.

But there was one young suitor who caught her eye, one boy her father would certainly have disapproved of, a young man not bred to wealth and position as she was. Whether her sudden infatuation was born of true emotion or merely a youthful desire to establish her independence from her father, Katherine was smitten.

She fell in love with this forbidden Romeo, like many a Juliet before and countless more after. The story might have begun as a fairy tale, but the ending was all too predictable, and it was not happily ever after. Her father discovered the secret affair of the two lovers and flew into a murderous rage. And Dr. Drish was not a man to be trifled with.

For four weeks, Dr. Drish locked his young daughter in her bedroom, permitting her only bread and water as sustenance. By the time she was finally released, her lover had disappeared from Tuscaloosa. She never saw him again. By what means Drish had disposed of him, whether fair or foul, he would take with him to his grave.

But Drish's victory was short-lived. Sadness and despair followed quickly, and when it came, it came to stay. The incident was the end of the stubborn and free-spirited Katherine. She died that day, for all practical purposes. She did not protest when her father gave her to be married to a gentlemen from New Orleans, a man of the wealth, birth and bearing that Dr. Drish demanded. The speculation and rumor among the old women of Tuscaloosa was that Katherine had been broken by her father, and even though the match produced two children, happiness never found her again.

No one can say when she began her descent into madness, but no one disputes that her fall was swift and certain. Eventually, when the signs became impossible to ignore or hide, her husband divorced her on grounds of insanity, sending her back to her father and the house that would become her hospital and her prison. Dr. Drish, though he had been a physician all his life, was not prepared to care for his own daughter. Instead of helping her, he merely locked her away. She remained confined largely to her room for the remainder of her sad days, her piano her only comfort. She would play for hours on end, stopping only when she became aware that someone was listening. Above all things, she loved flowers, and her father—perhaps regretting how he had treated her in her youth—kept her room filled with them in every variety. When she could escape into the outside world, she always returned with wildflowers to supplement those bought from the store.

The strain took a toll on the doctor's mental health, and like so many men before him, to drink and gambling he turned. His escapades became legendary throughout Tuscaloosa County and beyond. Local gossip held that he would often sell a fortune of cotton in Mobile only to lose it in a single night of poker.

The doctor's life had become a roller coaster of wild excess and deep depression. One of the few bright spots in his life came from his niece, Helen Whiting. The girl would often take extended visits to the mansion, staying for weeks at a time. Dr. Drish would pour all of the attention on her that he had once denied his invalid daughter and that she was now incapable of receiving. Surely the doctor was happy for once on the day he saw Helen married to a prominent and wealthy businessman in the area.

But whatever curse had fallen on Dr. Drish followed his niece to her marriage bed. She and her husband quarreled incessantly, and their fights were too often filled with vitriol and violence. It is said that the young girl's last words to her husband were, "Why, you know you would not hurt me. Now would you?" To which he replied, "I would not hurt a hair of your head." It was a promise he kept with meticulous cruelty. After the words had barely left his lips, he proceeded to sever her head from her body with a straight razor.

The husband was arrested and brought to trial, though like so many things in Dr. Drish's life, this too ended badly. Helen's erstwhile husband and murderer escaped the death penalty, claiming instead that insanity had seized him. Perhaps surprisingly, the courts agreed, and he was confined to an insane asylum. The confinement lasted only a few years. He moved away, married again and forgot about Helen and the Drish Mansion.

Between his daughter's growing insanity and Helen's things—many of which were still in the mansion from her many visits—Dr. Drish's drinking only intensified. His addiction eventually led to the failure of his business. That, of course, produced yet more drinking. The cycle of destruction continued until it came to its inevitable end.

One dark night, in the midst of a particularly devastating bout of delirium tremens, Dr. Drish burst from his bedroom and ran to the elegant curved stairway of his home. His shocked servants tried to pacify him, but they were unsuccessful. Dr. Drish uttered a horribly cry, as if he had seen into the very pit of hell, and fell dead on the spot. But he did not immediately leave the home he loved and to which he had dedicated his life's fortune. Instead of a traditional wake, his body was placed in the top tower room of the house, and his wife ensured that candles were burned there continually in his honor in the days leading up to his funeral.

But though his life was over, many believe that Dr. Drish's spirit did not rest. The stories began almost immediately following his passing. The servants dreaded the coming of the night, and often the family would awaken to the sound of a great cry, one of pain and death. Other times, the reverberations of heavy footsteps on the stairway would echo through the house, even if there were no living soul inside to make them.

The Widow Drish carried on, an elderly woman with an insane charge, locked in a house with nothing but her memories, too many of which were tragic. Katherine wandered from room to room, living in her own world, speaking in gibberish that only she could understand. Mrs. Drish did the best she could on the meager earnings she had left after her husband's debts were cleared, but soon she could no longer care for Katherine, and the girl's now adult sons came to take her away.

Nevertheless, wherever she went in life, some say Katherine returned to the mansion in death. To this day, even though the house has been abandoned for many decades, the overpowering smell of flowers is said to waft down from one of the upper bedrooms. And if one listens carefully, the tinkling of piano keys follows along with it, though it would surely end if one were able to find its source.

Sadly, Mrs. Drish did not last long after the untimely departure of the girl. Her dying wish was that her family light candles for her wake and honor her in the upper tower in the same way she had honored her husband. But the candles were never lit. Maybe her family believed it was a foolish request. Perhaps it was one that was simply forgotten in the preparations for the funeral. But whatever the case, the spirit of Mrs. Drish was apparently displeased by the slight. More than once, frightened neighbors alerted the authorities and local firemen, certain that the uppermost room of the mansion was on fire. But when the firefighters arrived, they invariably found no fire and no flames. No burning buildings. Just an unexplained false alarm.

The house passed from the Drish family to a long line of others—from the Cochranes to the Lilleys to the Snedecors—but the house's true owners never really left. The children who passed through the doors of the house spoke of an older woman who haunted the darkened hallways of their home. They would awake to her tucking them in at night or patting them gently on the head. The smell of flowers never left the upstairs bedroom, even when no flowers were present. Their nights were often interrupted by the sound of booming footsteps on the stairs or the terrified knockings of neighbors who swore the upper floors were on fire.

But the families never stayed, and eventually the house fell into disrepair. It passed to the Tuscaloosa Wrecking Company, where Walker Evans found it, and then became a school. It was almost destroyed by a local church that purchased the property, and even though that fate was averted by the efforts of the local historical society, the house remains in gloomy disrepair. While efforts are underway to restore it, funds are low, and the project is far from complete.

The only people who visit the Drish Mansion now are paranormal investigators, drawn by the stories of hauntings that have come down over the generations. They come seeking the spirits of Dr. Drish, his wife and poor Katherine. They rarely leave disappointed, their recording equipment filled with knocks and whispers, the tinkling of the piano and the booming of footsteps. The Drish Mansion may stand uninhabited, but it is not empty.

THE JEMISON–VAN DE GRAAFF MANSION

The story of the Drish Mansion would not be complete, however, without venturing down the road less than a mile to another of the great antebellum homes of Tuscaloosa—the Jemison–Van de Graaff Mansion. It was this Italianate-style home that legend says drove Dr. Drish to build his splendid plantation that would come to house so much grief and loss. And unfortunately, just as tragedy struck his house, so too would it come to the Jemison.

Constructed between 1859 and 1862, the house is named after the man who ordered its construction, Robert Jemison Jr. Jemison had a desire to build a grand showcase home, and he spared no expense on the house, hiring Philadelphia architect John Steward—who was in Tuscaloosa supervising the construction of what was then known as the Alabama Insane Hospital—as its chief designer. Having such a famed architectural genius at the helm guaranteed that the Jemison Mansion would transcend all that came before it and become the preeminent structure in Tuscaloosa, much to the chagrin of Dr. Drish.

The house was a modern marvel at the time, featuring running water, flushing toilets, coal gas–powered lighting and a gas stove. The Jemison Mansion would have contained even more technological wizardry, but the time of its construction could not have been worse. While it was truly the high-water mark of the Alabama economy, that period of prosperity was soon to be shattered by the greatest tragedy to ever strike our country. Secession, and with it the War Between the States, was on the winds, and as the Civil War began, so too did the Union blockade of Mobile Bay. The elaborate central heating plant that was meant to be installed in the Jemison Mansion to warm the grand conservatory never moved beyond the planning stages. It became just one of the great Civil War's many victims, if perhaps its least significant.

For his part, Robert Jemison had never been an avid Confederate and did not initially support secession. He had built his fortune after moving to Alabama in the 1820s, and his life was an early example of the fulfillment of the American dream. He started off modestly, purchasing small tracts of land until finally he had a sizable farm. He improved the land, adding industrial buildings including flour and gristmills. Jemison soon had his hands in a variety of businesses, investing in stagecoach lines, livery stables, a hotel and a thriving lumber and sawmill operation. With money came a desire to give back to the community he loved and to take political responsibility for its future. Jemison ran for public office, and in the 1830s, he entered the Alabama House of Representatives. He would soon graduate to the senate, where he became known as one of Alabama's most skilled politicians. There he worked to reform the state's lax business practices, going a long way to setting the state's financial affairs in order.

Who knows how far he might have gone in state and even national politics had war not come, but the problems that divided the country could no longer be salved with politics alone. With whispers of succession growing into full-throated shouts, Jemison tried to calm his colleagues in Montgomery, arguing against any efforts to leave the Union. In this endeavor, perhaps for the first time in his life, Jemison failed. The State of Alabama and its people were committed to the cause of Southern independence, and when the votes were tallied in Montgomery, the decision to abandon the Union was made once and for all. While Jemison did not support the action, he nevertheless accepted it wholeheartedly, pledging his loyalty to his state and the new nation of the Confederate States of America. The die was cast, and the South would burn for it.

According to legend, the fires of war very nearly took the Jemison Mansion as well. In August 1864, Union admiral David G. Farragut gave the now famous command, "Damn the torpedoes, full speed ahead!" during what would come to be known as the Battle of Mobile Bay. His words had barely

The Jemison Mansion.

faded before the Union army was on the march north. With Mobile taken, it was only a matter of time before the war came to Tuscaloosa as well. Union soldiers reached the city in April 1865, with only a few days remaining in the war. They took their vengeance there for the untold hardship and death they had faced, burning much of the University of Alabama in retribution. Next they turned their attention to punishing the man who had become Alabama's senator in the new Confederate government, Robert Jemison.

Jemison was warned that the Union authorities were looking for him, and he used the head start to hide in the swamps that surrounded his lands. Unable to find the man they hunted, the frustrated soldiers decided to burn the Jemison plantation to the ground. They destroyed much of Jemison's holdings before turning their attention to the mansion itself. Mrs. Jemison was given fifteen minutes to collect her things while Union soldiers with burning torches waited outside. A number of local boys took pity on the family, however. They put a plan in motion whereby they rode down the main streets of Tuscaloosa shouting, "Forrest is coming! Forrest is coming!" The Union soldiers, terrified by the prospect of facing the infamous Confederate cavalry commander, retreated to a fortified position. The Jemison Mansion was saved just in the nick of time.

The same could not be said for the majority of Robert Jemison's property. He had poured his fortune into the Confederate cause, and what had not been squandered during the war effort was thoroughly destroyed by the invading Union soldiers as militarily important targets. But while his fortune might have been in ruins, Jemison was not the kind of man who gave up easily. The South had to be rebuilt, and Jemison was just the person to do it.

Jemison poured himself into the reconstruction of the University of Alabama while also establishing a ferry service across the Black Warrior River. With the help of Horace King—a slave whose freedom Jemison had engineered in 1846 and who later became one of the most respected bridge builders in the South—Jemison's Tuscaloosa Bridge Company constructed bridges from Tuscaloosa to as far away as east Mississippi. By the time he passed away in the Jemison Mansion in October 1871, Jemison had reestablished himself to the point that he need not have feared that his beloved home would leave his family. Alas, the tragedy of the Civil War was only the first that would haunt the marbled halls of the mansion.

On December 5, 1865, Jemison's daughter, Cherokee, had taken a young lawyer named Andrew Hargrove to be her husband. Cherokee had received her unique name as a nod to family tradition. The story went that her grandparents gave Cherokee's mother, Priscilla, the middle name Cherokee in thanks to a local Indian chief who had saved their lives from an attack by another tribe. The name survives to the present day, having been passed down through at least six generations.

In any event, Andrew fell madly in love with Cherokee, and she was determined to have him. Unlike Dr. Drish, Robert Jemison had no interest in standing in the way of young love. Instead, he gave in to his daughter's wishes and consented to the two lovers' union, even though Andrew had lost much of his estate during the war.

His decision was based, at least in part, on Andrew's rather impressive background. A graduate of both Alabama and Harvard Law School, Andrew had only begun to practice law in Tuscaloosa when the war broke out. Like so many young men of his generation, he joined the Confederate army without hesitation, becoming an officer with an artillery battery.

For the first few years of the war, luck was with Robert, and he avoided injury. But in the summer of 1864, he was struck in the head by a Union bullet while trying to hold a river crossing over the Chattahoochee. The bullet cut a long gash across his forehead and was more significant for the wound's permanency than the actual damage it caused. He would carry a blue three-inch scar until the day he died.

It was a later incident, however, that would eventually lead to the events that cost Robert his life. In April 1865, just as the war was winding down and Rebel armies were collapsing around the South, Hargrove's unit engaged Union forces in Spanish Fort, Alabama. While trying to prevent their inevitable advance north, Hargrove was struck by a Minié ball just above his ear. Unlike the previous injury, this one was serious. The bullet pierced his skull into the brain. Hargrove was rushed into surgery, where doctors attempted to find the bullet and remove it, but as it was not on the outside of the skull, their efforts were judged more dangerous than merely leaving it alone. So there it remained, trapped somewhere inside Robert's brain.

For thirty years, Robert would carry that Minié ball with him in his brain, the excruciating headaches he suffered every day of his life a constant reminder of the horrors of war. For the decades that followed, Robert nevertheless managed the pain, rising to great prominence first as a local lawyer and then as an Alabama statesman. After working in the Constitutional Convention of the state in 1875, Robert would serve as a state senator before returning to the University of Alabama as a law professor. After several years as a popular teacher, he would rise to the position of law school dean.

But no matter the level of success he achieved, he could never fully leave the Civil War behind. The migraines that afflicted him daily grew worse as the years passed. Eventually, the pain simply became too much, and he could bear it no more. Finding no succor for his pain, he entered his library on December 6, 1895, thirty years and a day after he married Cherokee in the basement ballroom of the Jemison Mansion he now called home. There he put another bullet in his brain, though at least this one took away the suffering forever.

The same could not be said for his wife. Cherokee never recovered from her husband's suicide. Her crushing depression was followed by a swift descent into dementia and madness. She died in 1904, yet another victim of a war that had ended forty years before.

The mansion passed along Jemison's line, and in 1901, his most accomplished descendant, Robert Jemison Van de Graaff, was born there. Van de Graaff was somewhat of an inventive genius, a graduate of the University of Alabama who later worked at the Massachusetts Institute of Technology, where he designed a number of electrical devices, including the Van de Graaff generator (an example of which remains in the mansion to this day).

While Robert may have been the most renowned of the people born in the Jemison house—at least in Tuscaloosa, anyway—William T. "Bully" Van de Graaff is the most famous. Bully played the position of tackle for the University of Alabama football team. In 1915, Van de Graaff was the first University of Alabama Crimson Tide football player selected as an all-American. He was far from the last.

Following a period of disrepair and neglect, the Jemison Mansion served the city of Tuscaloosa as a library for a generation, before becoming the headquarters of *Antique Monthly* and *Horizon* magazines. The house is now under the ownership of the Jemison–Van de Graaff Mansion Foundation. But while no one lives in the mansion anymore, it does not sit empty.

One does not spend much time in the Jemison Mansion without experiencing something of the paranormal. One of the most common stories revolves around the apparition of a little girl. She lingers around the grand staircase of the mansion, and many visitors and employees have said they've seen or heard her; one even claims to have found the handprint of a child on a mirror in a closed-off room where no child could have been.

The historical records reveal no tragedy involving a young girl that might provide a reason for these manifestations. The best explanation for her appearance arises from a dark period when the Jemison Mansion fell into disrepair. In the 1930s, the family, like so many across the United States and the world, suffered from the ravages of the Great Depression. The house was sold and converted into an apartment building for low-income families. For almost ten years until 1945, the Jemison Mansion, with its two toilets and one bathtub, housed thirteen families. What once had been a house of luxury fell quickly into a home of squalor and disease. Would it be so surprising—in a time when life expectancies were low, especially for children—if the source of the lost little girl stemmed from that horrible time?

But the child is not the only spirit to haunt the halls of the Jemison Mansion. Some have claimed to have heard the sound of phantom music, one employee swearing to have recognized the strains of "Silent Night," even though it was the middle of the summer when the phantom song was played. Others claim to have heard heavy footsteps, even when there was no one else in the house. One of the most common occurrences is the sound of a great crash, as if a dozen china cabinets were violently thrown to the floor, all shattering glass and splintering wood. In one of the more famous stories, a wall mirror was thrown across an upper room, terrifying a young bride preparing for her wedding. Apparently, someone was unhappy with the commotion and disruption of the ceremony.

Brett had his own experience in the Jemison house during a paranormal investigation a few years past. His team had set up in the room where Robert Hargrove took his life a century ago. As they prepared to begin their investigation, Brett closed each of the doors in the room, checking them to make sure they were secure. Once they had settled, the leader of the investigation asked any entities that had joined them for a sign of their presence. At that moment, one of the doors Brett had secured swung open. He has no explanation—no scientific one at least—for this occurrence.

The Jemison Mansion is now a proud monument to Tuscaloosa's long and storied past. No doubt, most of the people who pass through its doors or who now rent the building for events are ignorant of the stories of specters that still haunt its halls. But like so many places in Tuscaloosa, in the Jemison Mansion, the past is not past. Rather, it and those who lived and died in days gone by are still very much present.

THE OLD TAVERN

Sitting on a hill within sight of downtown Tuscaloosa's main drag—but far enough away that only the most observant would notice it—is a structure that is one of the oldest in Tuscaloosa and indeed even in north Alabama. Reminiscent of the early French style that influenced much of southern architecture in the early nineteenth century, the building, with its brick façade and second-story overhanging balcony, looks as though it belongs on a winding street of New Orleans or a side alley of Mobile, if not in the heart of some Paris suburb.

In 1827, William Dunton, owner of the luxurious Golden Ball hotel in the formerly dusty stopover of Tuscaloosa that had grown into a burgeoning metropolis, opened an establishment that is known today as the Old Tavern. Dunton was a savvy businessman with an eye for a good deal, and he recognized that Tuscaloosa, recently named the state capital of Alabama, was on the verge of a boom. While the Golden Ball was meant for the well-to-do, the high-heeled and the wealthy, the Old Tavern catered to the less monetarily endowed traveler. With Tuscaloosa becoming a main stopover, it is no surprise that business was good. The location of the tavern didn't hurt either. Sitting along the main stagecoach route, any number of travelers passing through Tuscaloosa would have spent a weary night within its walls before continuing on their journeys.

Between 1826 and 1829, the tavern was located next door to a building that served as a temporary home for the state legislature. That convenience meant that in no time the tavern was doubling as a home away from home and meeting hall for state representatives. Soon, legislators were lodging there, as well as holding state committee meetings in the parlors. One of Alabama's early governors, John Gayle, even maintained a room in one of the cabins connected to the tavern during his administration. Who knows how many of Alabama's early laws were drafted and debated within its walls or how many state representatives engaged in scandalous dalliances there in secret. Even after the capitol moved down the street, many of the legislators continued to take their noon meals at the tavern, even until Montgomery became the capital in 1846.

While no doubt a blow to business, the tavern's colorful history did not end there. Like much of Alabama, it has its share of Civil War–inspired stories as well. As the war wound down, Confederate soldiers retreating from defeats in northern and southern Alabama would flee to the more central parts of the state, often staying at the tavern as they passed through Tuscaloosa. The entire family of Confederate general S.A.M. Woods is said to have sought refuge within its walls after the fall of Florence to the Federal army, renting both of the two large rooms on the upstairs level.

Luckily, the tavern survived the fires that burned much of the University of Alabama and damaged a good portion of downtown Tuscaloosa as well. The tavern served as a private residence for a while, but like so many of the great old buildings in Tuscaloosa, it fell into disrepair in the middle of the twentieth century, before eventually passing into the hands of the Tuscaloosa County Preservation Society. When the state decided to expand the Hugh Thomas Bridge over the Black Warrior River, the tavern faced destruction. Instead, in 1966, it was moved. The movement was a remarkable feat of community organization, with local schoolchildren raising money to fund the removal of the building to its present location, right next to the ruins of the old capitol—an appropriate resting place, given

Governor John Gayle's desk.

how inextricably the histories of the two old buildings are bound together. The Tuscaloosa County Preservation Society now runs the tavern as an office and museum of sorts, and it has become the terminus of a Tuscaloosa historical walking tour.

With all the souls that have passed through the Old Tavern's doors in its two hundred years of existence, it is no surprise that some of its guests have chosen not to leave. One of the most well-known stories involves the image of a human face—perhaps that of a child—on the panes of glass in the downstairs windows. Unlike similar phenomena reported in other haunted locations, the images are not permanent; rather, they arise only on certain nights. This lack of permanency has led some skeptics to suggest that the effect is simply the result of atmospheric changes affecting the clarity of the glass. Those who have witnessed the phenomenon, however, reject that explanation, claiming that what they witness is unlike any natural effect with which they are familiar. One compared the image to an oil slick moving across the surface of the water.

Whether a trick of the light or a legitimate supernatural phenomenon, the image on the glass is not the only unexplainable occurrence at the Old Tavern. The sound of stumbling footsteps is occasionally heard echoing down the main stairway. Anyone who has ever visited the building undoubtedly was struck by the winding, narrow staircase consisting of steps of different heights and angles that is virtually impossible to climb without losing one's footing. The story goes that the tavern's builder, William Dunton, being a man whose success was well known, was notoriously paranoid about intruders sneaking up on him in the middle of the night and stealing his money. The design of the staircase ensured that no one could walk up the steps without stumbling and making noise, a fact that is clear to anyone who has ever tried to climb the stairs. Apparently, even the dead have this trouble.

While the Old Tavern has many stories of the supernatural associated with it, one of the more humorous tales revolves around a peculiar piece of furniture that is not native to the tavern but is now housed there: Mims Jemison's rocking chair. Jemison, no relation to the Jemisons who owned the Jemison Mansion, is said to have crafted a special rocking chair with one particularly amusing feature. Only Jemison knew how to properly use the chair, and anyone else who tried to sit on it would always fall over. Jemison is said to have taken advantage of this feature to hilarious effect. He would leave his chair behind with an excuse that he needed something in another room, specifically telling anyone in the room not to sit in his chair. Invariably, someone would put old Jemison to the test, and the sound of the

Above: The Old Tavern.

Left: Mims Jemison's haunted rocking chair.

chair crashing to the floor would be outshone only by Jemison's cackling from the other room. While the days of Jemison's practical jokes are long gone, perhaps he has found another way to amuse himself. More than once, a visitor to the Old Tavern has witnessed the chair move of its own accord with no apparent explanation.

The Old Tavern provides a unique window into a time when Tuscaloosa was just coming into its own as a major Alabama city, a time of transition between dusty stopover to state capital and later victim of the Civil War. They say that to this day, there is a draw to the lonely structure, that visitors who have never before been to the city often find themselves on its doorstep, even if they know nothing of its story and have no idea what purpose it once served. The Old Tavern has always had that draw, and it is one that just might extend beyond the mortal plane.

THE BATTLE-FRIEDMAN HOUSE

While the Jemison Mansion and the Drish Mansion are probably the most famous of the renowned antebellum homes in Tuscaloosa, they are by no means the oldest. The Battle-Freidman House, on the other hand, is certainly in contention for that honor, and it is no doubt one of the most beautiful homes in the city. And while some of the spirits that are said to haunt Tuscaloosa's other famous residences might be best avoided, it seems to be a friendly ghost that calls the Battle-Friedman House home.

Built in 1835 by Alfred Battle and his wife, Millicent, what was then known as the Battle House consisted of two front parlors divided by a central hallway with a second floor of rooms resting above. The distinctive square-box columns were added in those heady days of optimism preceding the Civil War, as were the rooms in the back of the house. The exterior has the appearance of red marble, an illusion created by placing stucco over brick and then painting it. Meant to be a symbol of the Battles' wealth and success, the house was built with the intention that it should occupy an entire city block. One of the benefits of this extra space was the construction of what is now the only remaining antebellum garden in the state.

Alfred Battle was originally from North Carolina and was the son of a wealthy family in the area. Unfortunately for Alfred, he was not the oldest son, and what is now an insignificant fact was then of utmost importance. Due to the customs that held sway at the time, Alfred was basically left to

The Battle-Friedman House, front view.

his own devices when it came to establishing his legacy. His older brother was due to inherit the family's land, and Alfred decided it would be better to leave the state of North Carolina behind and pursue his fortune in some other place. That place turned out to be Tuscaloosa, Alabama. He found that fortune in a perhaps unlikely but not uncommon place: Millicent's dowry, which Alfred used to buy a farm in the southern part of the state. But Alfred was more than just a gold digger. He quickly used his skills to turn that farm into a cotton plantation, making both himself and Millicent incredibly wealthy. In fact, the Tuscaloosa mansion, which strikes the casual observer as a stately antebellum plantation house, was originally only the family's town home; they owned a bigger and even more impressive house out of town. Over the years, though, the family came to spend more and more of their time in the city, and the house expanded according to their needs.

The Battles were particularly doting on their son, William Augustus Battle. Not surprisingly, they initially celebrated when William courted and married Susanna Clay Withers from Huntsville, Alabama. The celebration was short-lived, however, when Susanna showed a penchant for lavish spending. Where Alfred had built his fortune through frugality and good business sense, the young couple built a colossal mansion down the street from the Battle House, overspending wildly on its construction, perhaps in an effort to outshine the home of the old man. The conclusion of construction did not bring financial restraint, however, and when the economic panic of 1857 gripped the nation, Susanna and William were in no way prepared for it. They suffered greatly at its hands, and in its wake, they lost their mansion and were forced to move in with Alfred and Millicent. The latter used this opportunity to restore control over Susanna, and the young woman was forced to reform her hitherto excessive ways.

One of the more famous figures to reside in the Battle House was Virginia Clay Clompton. Virginia was the niece of Alfred and, after the death of her parents, was raised by him as the daughter he never had. William and Virginia certainly fought like siblings, with Virginia ripping out a chunk of his hair during one particularly vicious spat. In his later years, William would often joke that his sister had scalped him. We might not know of this anecdote had Virginia not become a rather well-respected author. Later in her life, she recorded the story in her memoirs, *A Belle of the Fifties*. Virginia certainly had a story to tell. In the days following the end of the Civil War, she and her husband were accused of joining in the plot to assassinate Abraham Lincoln. Virginia might very well have been executed for that crime like many of the other accused, but fortune, and perhaps family connections, smiled on her. She spent nearly a year imprisoned in Fort Monroe, Virginia, and was freed only after President Andrew Johnson himself ordered her release in 1866.

As for the Battle House, it remained in the Battle family until 1875, when Bernard Friedman purchased the home for himself. Friedman was a self-made man, having emigrated from Europe in his youth. Upon arriving in America, he began a business selling clothing, mostly whatever wares he could carry on his back or in the little cart he pulled behind him. But Friedman was driven, and his story was the sort that embodied the American dream of immigrants around the world. What started as a small operation eventually grew to include a chain of clothing stores. By the time he purchased the Battle House from a now war-ravaged and struggling family, he had become quite wealthy.

The house passed along his line until, in 1965, Hugo Friedman willed the home to the City of Tuscaloosa. Hugo was a close friend of legendary University of Alabama football coach Paul "Bear" Bryant and was known for his great charity toward the city and university. It is thus not surprising that one of his last acts was to donate the house to posterity.

The Battle-Friedman House is currently operated by the Tuscaloosa Country Preservation Society. Due to its beauty and a general air of welcome that hangs about the grounds, the Battle-Friedman House is a popular destination for weddings and other celebrations in the area.

Like many of the great old houses of Tuscaloosa, Battle-Friedman has a haunted history to go along with its more conventional one. But while the spirits that haunt some of the other locations in this book are occasionally frightening, the ghosts of Battle-Friedman seem to be of the more protective variety. The common thread that ties them all together is a love for the home and a desire to protect it.

The spirits of both Suzanna Clay and Adele Friedman are said to remain behind in the house. In fact, the docents who take care of the home have reported seeing evidence of their presence. Specifically, they have found wet footprints in the bathroom (which they watched dry before their eyes) and footprints in the dust beneath a chair. There was no one in the house at the time who could have left those marks. Another reminder of the women comes in the form of old-fashioned floral perfume that visitors have reported wafting through the corridors of the house. Furniture is occasionally rearranged during the night, and the docents have reported hearing the sound of people doing chores in rooms where no living souls reside.

But it's not just the humans who didn't want to leave the Battle-Friedman House behind. Hugo Friedman had a pet collie, which is also reported to roam the home. In life, the dog was known to be extraordinarily affectionate and loving. Death did not rob it of that attribute. Those who have stayed in the house have reported feeling the dog in bed with them at night, along with a sense of general comfort. And that seems to be the overall perception of most of the visitors to the Battle-Friedman House. None claims to feel a sense of oppression when visiting the home. Rather, they all experience a sensation of welcome and protection. Apparently, southern hospitality can survive even the grave.

JEMISON CENTER (OLD BRYCE INSANE ASYLUM)

Haunted sites in Tuscaloosa are in no short supply. And given the city's historical significance, neither are interesting and mysterious locations. That the two often go hand in hand is no surprise. But every now and then, the legends that grow up around a place outrun the history. Old Bryce—famous to teenagers, college students and ghost hunters alike as an ancient, abandoned insane asylum filled with horrific secrets—is one of those places.

The Stories of Tuscaloosa

On the outskirts of the town of Northport—Tuscaloosa's sister city that lies across the Warrior River—sits an abandoned antebellum-style building. It is little more than a ruin today, having suffered extensive fire damage in addition to the normal wear and tear one would expect. There's graffiti, broken windows and wild animal infestation. The house lies at the end of a long, broken driveway shaded by ancient, gnarled oak trees. The end of the driveway circles around an empty fountain, so bone dry that one wonders if water ever flowed there. Even though the location is only a few hundred yards from houses and the highway, a preternatural silence lies over the countryside. Standing in that absence of sound, it feels as though you are as far as could be from human civilization.

And yet, one can imagine the beauty that must have been there once, back before decay and destruction came to Old Bryce. When the road was new and undamaged, when the trees were not so twisted, when the antebellum columns were a shining white and when crystal-clear water flowed freely from the stone fountain that stands before the old asylum. Yes, standing there in the shadow of the slowly disintegrating structure, you can almost see it and almost hear it. There was a time when the complex was almost

Jemison Center.

beautiful, if a place that housed the mentally ill—the too-often-forgotten outcasts of our society—can be called beautiful. But if you believe the stories that people tell about the place, sometimes you don't have to imagine what it might have been like at Old Bryce all those years ago. The spirits are there to remind you.

The land on which Old Bryce sits once belonged to the famous Jemison family. It was Jemison who laid out the approach to the home, planted the oak trees that now flank the long drive and constructed the building and the fountain that lie at its end. Around the same time, Jemison constructed a vacation home on the plot of quiet land away from the city, as well as a home for his in-laws nearby. Upon his death, Jemison gave the property as a bequest to the State of Alabama Board of Mental Health.

While the antebellum style and ancient oaks have led to the common appellation of "Old Bryce" for the facility, it is more properly known as the Jemison Center, named in honor of Jemison's generosity. The facility itself is more myth and legend than reality. The actual Bryce Hospital on the campus of the University of Alabama is far older than the Jemison

Jemison Center Main entrance.

Center, which was built in 1939. While presented by most visitors as an insane asylum, Jemison was actually built as a school for mentally retarded and handicapped boys. It served as a dormitory for patients and the boys who worked on the farmlands that surround the center, and the home itself has more in common with a boarding school than a mental hospital. The facility had a bakery, a laundromat, a warehouse and a dairy, all of which were worked by the patients. And despite rumors that the hospital closed as a result of nefarious practices or secret experiments, in reality, it was lax funding, not lax morals, that led to the facility's closure. Which is not to say that conditions at the home were ideal. The funding issues that beset Alabama's mental health program often led to shockingly poor conditions. It took one of the largest and longest federal lawsuits in history to alleviate the situation.

But whatever the reality of the Jemison Center's history, it has done nothing to squelch the growth of dark tales and whispered rumors about the spirits that haunt its halls. There's a notion in popular culture that the insane have unstable or troubled spirits. When you add that feeling to the

A view inside Jemison Center.

Jemison Center's main staircase.

natural horror of insane asylums, it is no surprise that people tend to have paranormal experiences in mental institutions. Stories from the Jemison run the gamut. People have heard voices, had their hair pulled or felt as though they were punched or kicked. Others claim that the sound of piano music sometimes wafts through the halls, and still other visitors grow instantly sick upon entering the building. Doors slam, footsteps echo through floors where no one should be and the smell of antiseptic or new bandages appears in rooms left to the elements for decades.

Do these stories have any basis in reality? It is almost impossible to say. Universally, those students, paranormal investigators and even old staff who have experienced the bizarre occurrences at Old Bryce consistently report that strange and paranormal activity are the norm not the exception. Perhaps these reports are merely the result of overactive imaginations. Maybe there is nothing at Old Bryce but a seemingly ancient building that is crumbling into dust, surrounded by overgrown weeds and gnarled trees that only added to the mysteriousness of the location. That is possible. Certainly, the reality of Jemison Center does not match the legend of Old Bryce, but who can say what brings paranormal activity and what does not? Perhaps there is something we do not know about Old Bryce that would explain what so many people have experienced. Maybe there is some mystery there just waiting to be uncovered, one whose truth would explain all.

Maybe. But whatever the truth may be, Jemison Center remains a place of mystery and foreboding for the people of Tuscaloosa and Northport. That's the sort of thing you can only feel, even if you can't really explain it.

THE SHIRLEY HOUSE

The subject of paranormal activity always has and always will stir passions and debate. Whether ghosts, spirits or poltergeists even exist is hotly disputed, though those who have experienced one of these phenomena first hand have no such doubts. And even if we accept the existence of paranormal phenomena, the questions don't end there. Are spirits really the disembodied essence of the dead? Are they some sort of psychic resonance left over from some past age? Are they the result of traumatic events so horrible that they are burned into the fabric of reality? Or are they simply malfunctions in the brain caused by overstimulation from stray electromagnetic fields?

And yet, even if we could settle on one of these explanations, we still would not know why some locations are haunted while others are not. Places where violent deaths have occurred are obvious candidates for a haunting, but what to make of places like the Bama Theatre, where no one has died and yet paranormal activity is rampant? Sometimes, it seems as though the activity is most directly related to a particular object. Such is the case of the Shirley House in Northport, just across the river from Tuscaloosa, where the past seems most present around an old schoolmaster's desk from the nineteenth century.

The Shirley House was constructed in 1837. The brick raised cottage in Northport served as the home of James Shirley, an early settler to the state of Alabama who originally hailed from South Carolina. Shirley was himself a builder and developer, and he had a hand in constructing many of the early residences and commercial buildings in Northport. The home remained in the family until 1997, when Shirley's great-nephew, Marvin Harper, deeded the house to the City of Northport to create a Heritage and Learning Center.

Perhaps there would be nothing more to the story of the Shirley House than that were it not for a mid-1850s pine and tulip wood schoolmaster's

The Shirley House.

desk now located in the downstairs den. The desk itself is an interesting piece of American history. In the nineteenth century, schooling was not an organized enterprise. There were no school districts, no school boards or superintendents and no centralized educational system. There were no state tests or federal oversight. Instead, those parents who could afford to educate their children did so in the home.

The desk that now resides in the Shirley House was known as a schoolmaster's desk. Ordinarily, a plantation owner would designate one of the rooms in his home as a schoolroom. He would then hire a teacher who would instruct the children for about half the year. The desk was provided for the teacher by the plantation owner.

The particular desk in the Shirley House is a combination of desk and bookshelf and stands almost six feet tall. Two sturdy wooden doors cover the bookcase, while the writing section was slanted toward the occupant. The slanted section could lift up, revealing a storage area underneath. The desk was originally in a plantation in Mississippi before it made its way to the Shirley House.

Throughout the years, the desk has been the center of paranormal activity in the house, possibly related to some unknown event that occurred while it was still in Mississippi. Whatever the cause, the residents and workers at the Shirley House agree that there's something off with the old wooden piece of furniture. The heavy wooden doors are known to move of their own accord, and one witness claims that not a single day goes by that they don't hear the rattling sound of the doors swinging open and closed.

One might assume at first blush that such occurrences would be frightening at worst and severely unsettling at best, but that's not how those who have experienced them firsthand describe the phenomena. Rather, they claim there is something comforting about the presence, as if it is watching over them, and that as long as it is around, nothing bad would happen. Perhaps it is the essence of whatever schoolteacher once owned the desk still protecting his charges a full century after his death.

The writing desk in the Shirley House gets most of the attention, but there is another spirit that many claim still haunts its halls—that of Elizabeth Shirley. Elizabeth was the mother of James Shirley, builder of the house. As was common at the time, in her elderly years Elizabeth came to live with James in his home in Northport. In fact, she lived in the house with Shirley from the time it was built until her death in 1865. Her bedroom on the second floor of the house is called the Elizabeth Shirley Room to this day. Visitors to the home often hear footsteps in the upstairs bedroom. Others have heard voices calling their names from inside the room, only to find it empty upon inspection.

But while footsteps and phantom voices are often encountered in supposedly haunted locations, the Shirley House has something even more intriguing—a full-bodied apparition believed to be Elizabeth. Marvin Harper, the descendant of Elizabeth Shirley who eventually donated the house to the city, reported that a guest of his saw Elizabeth standing at the foot of her bed. She described the apparition as not threatening but rather a beautiful image of a lady from sometime in the past. She claimed to have seen the apparition again that same night.

Despite believing he lived with two spirits, Marvin Harper claimed he was never afraid while in the Shirley House. Rather, he felt protected and comforted. The spirits, he said, were simply taking care of the home they loved so well in their lives. That's not a bad fate at all.

BAMA THEATRE

In the middle of downtown Tuscaloosa, in the center of a part of town that is experiencing remarkable revitalization, sits a structure that was at its height the last time the downtown area was booming. Strange things are said to happen there. Doors slam shut. Elevators move up and down with no passengers and no purpose. A hound dog bays in the basement. Whispers waft through hallways, and words echo in the distance. At the Bama Theatre, for some patrons at least, it is always show time.

The Bama Theatre is a local landmark. Constructed in 1937 and opened in April 1938 during the depths of the Great Depression, the Bama Theatre was built as part of Franklin Delano Roosevelt's New Deal. From the moment it was announced, the Bama Theatre was a source of hope and excitement for a population that was in short supply of both. And from the beginning, the Public Works Administration project was quite an undertaking.

Designed by Birmingham architect D.O. Whildin, the Bama Theatre was one of the last great movie palaces built in the South. Art Deco styling on the exterior melds with an interior design based on those popular in Spain during the century before. The Bama Theatre also has a touch of Italy, as much of the interior is a reproduction of the courtyard of the Davanzati Palace in Florence. Painted stars and clouds complete the illusion, and one can imagine himself enjoying an open-air performance during the height of the Renaissance era.

All told, the complex cost $200,000 to complete, a royal sum at the time. It was the first public building in the city of Tuscaloosa to include air conditioning. The opening of the Bama Theatre was practically a holiday in the city. The University of Alabama's Million-Dollar Band even led a parade. The first movie shown in the Bama was *Million-Dollar Baby*, starring Cary Grant and Katherine Hepburn. At its height, the Bama drew an audience of nearly nine hundred people to a single performance.

As the grand movie palaces gave way to the multiplexes of today, the Bama Theatre was forced to adapt. It was converted into a performing arts center in the 1970s and was completely renovated to host live performances. Today, it regularly hosts both local and touring performances, as well as showing classic, foreign and art house films.

The source of the Bama Theatre's paranormal reputation is somewhat of a mystery. Researchers have been able to find no evidence of suicide or murder. And unlike many of the other great theaters throughout the country, there was never a fire at the Bama that cost lives. No one fell from a

Bama Theatre.

balcony to his death there, and there have been no mysterious deaths related to some mid-summer's eve performance of *Macbeth*. Yet there can be no denying that something wicked—or at least paranormal—has come to the Bama Theatre.

In many ways, the Bama Theatre exhibits what might be called the prototypical indicia of a haunting. Universally, the employees at the Alabama theater talk about feeling as though they are never alone. They hear noises they shouldn't hear, like the sound of thunder from stage plays long since dead. They see figures and shadows walking down the hallways and up the aisles when the theater is otherwise empty. Several of the theater's staff members have reported seeing mysterious shadows walking in front of the usher lights when the stage is dark. Some have described being terrified to be alone in the building.

Perhaps the most intriguing phenomena associated with the Bama Theatre centers on the building's elevators. In the middle of the night, when all is quiet, the roar of the elevator can be heard as it turns on of its own accord. The sound itself is unsettling, but some employees have experienced even more bizarre events. One former director was known as a pragmatic, down-to-earth guy; some of the staff at the Bama Theatre even referred to him as overly serious and lacking a sense of humor. He had a habit of getting to the theater early in the morning. One day, as he was making coffee, he heard the elevator start up. It traveled to the top level, stopped and then went back down to the second floor where he was waiting, just outside the doors. The elevator dinged, and the doors opened. That's when the real terror began. The director described it as a burst of freezing cold air, like a gale had erupted from inside the elevator and yet somewhere beyond, somewhere that was icy cold. He claimed the temperature dropped forty degrees in those few seconds. He never went in early to the theater again.

Animals appear to be particularly attuned to whatever haunts the Bama. One staff member brought his wife and dogs to the theater to set up for a show the next day. The two dogs were on the stage, playing around, doing what dogs do, when suddenly they stopped. The older dog, Jake, went to the edge of the stage and stared out into the seats. He started wagging his tail, as if he saw someone. The dog ran down the stage and up the aisle. But halfway up, something changed. Jake came to a dead stop. His tail stopped wagging. He turned then, running to the stage door with his tail between his legs, pawing at it and whimpering, begging for escape from whatever it was he saw. To this day, Jake won't go back into the theater.

The Bama Theatre remains a source of pride and joy for the people of Tuscaloosa, and today, it is perhaps more successful than it has ever been. But when the lights go down and the stage goes dark, that's when the show really starts. According to many who have experienced parts of that play, the subject is most assuredly horror, and the actors are no longer of this world.

GREENWOOD CEMETERY

Located off the beaten path on the outskirts of downtown Tuscaloosa, Greenwood Cemetery is one of the oldest and most important cemeteries in all of Tuscaloosa County. Laid out in 1821—though burials began as early as 1818—many of the city's most important leaders were laid to rest within its confines. These leading lights include Dr. John Drish, the Stillmans (after whom a local college is named), two generals of the Confederate army and the only Confederate soldier killed during the Battle of Tuscaloosa and subsequent burning of the University of Alabama. It is undoubtedly a historical treasure, one often studied by scholars from local schools and those around the country.

In many ways, the cemetery, like any burying ground, mirrors the living world of the era in which it was constructed. African American graves are segregated from those of white people, and even Native Americans lie within its confines. The socioeconomic class of the deceased is readily ascertainable from the state of the grave itself. Many of the graves of the poorest have no markers at all, at least not with names. Simple bricks stand in for the more ostentatious memorials to the city's wealthier inhabitants.

Part of the cemetery has a high percentage of babies and children buried within. These markers are a reminder of a cholera epidemic that swept through Tuscaloosa in the 1800s. The disease killed indiscriminately, but the heaviest burden fell on the young.

There are also a great number of veterans of the Revolutionary War, as well as Civil War casualties, buried within Greenwood. Some have even speculated that Confederate gold is buried within the confines of the graveyard, and more than once the police have been called to chase off would-be treasure hunters. It is the kind of place where one can marvel at the great marble crypts of lost antiquity and where one can still find the name of the man who carved a grave marker on the bottom of the tombstone.

But it is not the historical significance alone that brings visitors to the Greenwood Cemetery. For while it may be a city of the dead, not all lie peacefully within its confines, and the stories of those who still walk within its walls are well known to the people of Tuscaloosa.

Some speak of an old man who once worked on one of the riverboats that plied their trade on the Black Warrior River. In his spare time, the man played the banjo, and his reputation for having extraordinary ability was known throughout the county. Death did not silence his instrument, and the sound of distant banjo music is often heard wafting among the tombstones.

Others have seen the ghost of twelve-year-old Virginia Summers walking between the tombstones, playing hide-and-seek within the maze of the cemetery. Like so many of the spirits of Tuscaloosa, her story goes back to the Civil War. Confederate soldiers were marching through Tuscaloosa on parade, and Virginia desperately wanted to see them in action. Her parents refused, of course, but that didn't stop Virginia from riding her pony downtown. But between the sights and sounds and great warhorses of the Confederate army, the small pony was spooked. It threw young Virginia from its back, and she hit her head on the hard cobblestone street. The town doctors did all they could to save her, but it was to no avail. She died, and

Tombstone of Virginia Hanna Summers.

her final resting place is in Greenwood. To this day, the specter of a little girl in nineteenth-century clothing is seen skipping through the cemetery, as if in excitement to witness some grand event, by people of all walks of life. But she never makes it beyond the tombstone of Virginia Summers.

The ghost of Abby Snow is also said to haunt the graveyard. She is one of the victims of the great cholera epidemic that killed so many in Tuscaloosa, dying at the age of only ten months in 1844. She is known as the crying child, and the sound of her sorrow is often heard around her tombstone. At least Abby is remembered. Many children whose names are long lost to history are seen playing in the cemetery, eternal reminders of the disease that left so many mothers and fathers to mourn the passing of their young ones.

James MacLester, a child of fifteen, began to appear after a statue was stolen from his grave. Those who knew him from life were said to easily recognize him. Apparently, he searches for the stolen statue, forever seeking to return it to his grave, where it belongs.

More than one mourner has witnessed soldiers marching around the graves of Confederate dead at night, while others report the presence of a

Above: Tombstone of Abby Myra Snow.

Below: Tombstone of James Henry McLester.

spectral hound that is said to have belonged to an Indian warrior. Others see floating, ghostly lights of the old innkeeper who used to walk through the cemetery at night. The light has confounded more than one caretaker who searched to no avail for the grave robbers who carried that infernal lantern.

Many in the city of Tuscaloosa simply shun the old cemetery, their fear overcoming their curiosity for the historical site. Death is ever-present there, remembered in stone and perhaps by something far less of this world.

THE MURPHY-COLLINS HOUSE

The long history of segregation and discrimination throughout the United States is well known, but many times the stories of those pioneers who broke through the barriers are forgotten. Mr. William J. Murphy is one of those people, and in Tuscaloosa, the Murphy Museum stands as a tribute to his life.

The Murphy-Collins House is unique in all of the historical buildings in Tuscaloosa. It is the only building constructed in the twentieth century that is presently designated by the Tuscaloosa Country Preservation Society as a historically significant property. And no wonder. The Murphy-Collins House has quite a history.

Built in a time when segregation affected not only water fountains and restrooms but also the planning of entire cities, the Murphy-Collins House stands on the corner of Paul W. Bryant Drive and Lurleen Wallace Boulevard in what would have been known as the "colored section" of Tuscaloosa. This was part of an area downtown where the majority of the African American residents resided. The reasons for the segregation were partially legal and partially social. Many majority-white sections in town required that their property deeds include a specific clause forbidding the sale of the land or house to minorities. In fact, while these clauses have long since been found void in the courts as discriminatory, many deeds still include them, unbeknownst to the current owners.

In any event, few African Americans challenged the status quo in the early part of the century, whether in court or otherwise. While the presence and power of the Ku Klux Klan is often overstated, its dangerous hand, as well as that of other racist organizations, was certainly felt and feared at the time, and stepping out of line could be dangerous to one's health and that of one's family, as well.

The Murphy-Collins House actually sat on what might be called the border of the black and white areas of town. In fact, the front of the house faced a row of white owned and occupied buildings. Looking out his front window, Mr. Murphy was literally looking across the border of segregation in the city of Tuscaloosa.

Because of its proximity to the white part of town, the Murphy-Collins House was one of the nicer homes occupied by African Americans at the time, and it and its neighbors would have housed middle-class black professionals. Thus, the house depicts a lifestyle of which we are often ignorant in the modern day—that of the wealthier but still discriminated against black middle class.

The house was built in 1923 by Mr. Will J. Murphy and his wife. Mr. Murphy employed a fellow African American named George Clopton to build the two-story home. Like a surprising number of structures built at the time, Murphy and Clopton salvaged bricks and beams from the ruins of what had been the Alabama State Capitol Building. While the old capitol had survived the ravages of the Civil War intact, it could not survive the combination of a simple fire and inadequate city fire protection.

The citizens of Tuscaloosa were not shy about taking what they could from the site, and Murphy acquired the material he needed to build the home for a mere $900. The house had two fireplaces to fight the cold, one on each floor, but like most homes built at the time, it did not have indoor plumbing. It was only a few years ago that a bathroom was added off the back porch to replace the outhouse.

The reason Murphy was able to build his house in what was considered the nicer part of the segregated African American section of Tuscaloosa had much to do with his acumen as a businessman. Murphy was the first African American licensed to practice as an embalmer and mortician in the city of Tuscaloosa. Because of this distinction, he was able to become the preeminent funeral home director in all of Tuscaloosa County and beyond. In total, he owned four separate businesses in Tuscaloosa, and in 1916, he acquired the entire stock of the Tuscaloosa Undertaking Company.

Upon his death, the Murphy-Collins House passed to his wife, Laura Murphy, the principal of the Twentieth Street School for African American children. It then passed on to Mr. Murphy's nephew. The nephew eventually sold the home to Mrs. Sylvia Collins, thus giving the home its second name. As the years passed, urban renewal projects threatened the Murphy-Collins House, and in fact many other homes of historical significance fell to the gradual march of time and progress. At some point, however, the City of Tuscaloosa, inspired by the work of concerned citizens who realized the significance of the Murphy-Collins House and the need to preserve the contributions of African Americans to the city, decided to purchase the home. The city then designated it as a place to be used for the historical preservation and exhibition of African American heritage and culture.

Today, the home has been restored and renovated to its prior glory and beauty. Under the control of the Tuscaloosa County Preservation Society, the home is now designated the Murphy African American Museum. It contains a diverse and varied collection of black memorabilia and serves as a testament to the contributions of African Americans around the country, with a focus on the city of Tuscaloosa and the state of Alabama as a whole.

The collection contained in the Murphy Museum is quite impressive and features a number of items from the African continent, including African masks and artwork. It also chronicles the inventive genius of African Americans throughout history. These include the well-known works of George Washington Carver, as well as lesser-known men such as Elijah McCoy and Garret A. Morgan.

McCoy is probably known as much for his contribution to the English language as for his patents and engineering marvels. McCoy, the son of parents who had fled from the slaveholding South via the Underground

The Murphy-Collins House.

Railroad to Canada, studied engineering in Scotland and earned the title of master mechanic and engineer. While he was unable to get a job equal to his qualifications because of widespread discrimination, McCoy did not let that stop him from succeeding at his endeavors. During his career, McCoy patented more than fifty of his inventions. Counterfeiting was a serious problem at the time, however, and it is said that salesman would assure customers that their products were legitimate by calling them "the real McCoy."

Garrett A. Morgan was also an inventor, one responsible for saving untold lives in World War I. In 1916, an explosion trapped over thirty men in a tunnel 250 feet below ground. Morgan led a group of volunteers to save the men, but poisonous gasses had filled the tunnel where they were trapped. Fortunately, Morgan used his inventive genius to fashion a gas mask that allowed his party to rescue the men. The U.S. Army took notice and ordered Morgan gas masks for the troops serving in Europe, where poisonous gas was being used as a weapon for the first time. Perhaps more famously, Morgan was responsible for the first version of the traffic signal used in North America.

While these men certainly hold a special place in the Murphy-Collins House, it is not just inventors who are honored in the Murphy Museum. Musicians, artists, businessmen and civil rights leaders are also remembered. In fact, the museum has become a popular stop along the Civil Rights Trail that leads from Selma to Montgomery, up through Tuscaloosa and on to Birmingham. The museum helps to document the struggles of African Americans under segregation. While Alabama has its share of shame from that period of time, the civil rights era is also a great time of triumph for the state, and the Murphy Museum marks that triumph.

All told, the Murphy Museum is a remarkable monument to the great African American men and women in United States history, including Mr. Murphy himself. The past is very much alive within its walls. According to those who know best, some of that history is still present, making itself known in strange and unexpected ways.

The docents who oversee the Murphy-Collins House are adamant that the house does not sit empty. One spirit in particular they have seen evidence of time and again. They call this specter the "water ghost." According to the ladies who work in the home, whenever it rains, puddles of waters—like footprints—appear on the floor. There is no sign of a leak, no wet spots on the ceiling or the walls. Many times, those puddles simply disappear without anyone having to clean up the spills. It is as if whatever made the small puddles feels bad about leaving a mess behind and seeks to clean it up. People have tried to ascertain a normal, ordinary source of the water, but so far they have been unsuccessful.

They have also heard the sounds of people walking around the house, even at night when the docents are by themselves. Sometimes it is the sound creaking, which might be dismissed as merely the house settling. But other times, the unmistakable sound of footsteps echoes through the hallways. If the ladies who work in the house look for the source, though, the sound disappears, and they find nothing. Normally, these sounds come from the scientists and inventors' room.

Footsteps are also heard in the upstairs bedroom, particularly in Mr. Murphy's old room. The closet door opens on its own in that bedroom, frightening the ladies who spend the most time in the house. Still, the ladies say that they don't feel an evil presence with them in the home. Instead, it seems that perhaps the Murphys are still deeply proud of their accomplishments in life, as well as the monument their home became after their deaths. It is no surprise, really. The Murphy Museum is a fitting tribute to one of Tuscaloosa's true pioneers.

MAXWELL'S CROSSING

Most ghost stories revolve around a building or a structure—old insane asylums, hospitals, antebellum homes, university classrooms through whose halls a couple centuries of students have passed, that sort of thing. I suppose it is no real surprise. After all, people spend the vast majority of their time in their homes and businesses, and many people end their lives there. The same is true of hospitals and insane asylums, with the latter especially being the location of some of the worst experiences a human being could ever endure.

But while most haunted places are buildings, some of the most legendary— and allegedly most spiritually active—are simply some spot in an open field. That is the case with a little spot of myth and legend outside Tuscaloosa city proper known simply as Maxwell's Crossing.

The closest populated area is that of Maxwell, about two miles away from the crossing. Maxwell's Crossing itself is barely more than a dirt road, hardly wide enough for two vehicles to pass each other at one time. But despite that fact, Maxwell's Crossing is universally known by the people who live nearby as a hotbed for paranormal activity of all sorts, including poltergeists, ghosts and even the occasional UFO or alien encounter.

While Maxwell's Crossing has any number of stories, there's one that every young couple from the Tuscaloosa area is well aware of. It is said that along the dirt road that constitutes Maxwell's Crossing are thirteen wooden bridges. Untold numbers of boys and girls from the area have traveled down that dirt road, counting the bridges as they drove, one through thirteen. At the end of the road, the couple must make a u-turn. While driving back down the dirt road to the highway, the couple is then to attempt the seemingly innocuous task of counting the bridges again. Invariably, they will only count twelve.

What explains this mysterious discrepancy? In truth, it has never been fully explained. Some speculate that it is a hoax altogether, but too many people (including the authors) have attempted—and failed—to count the same number of bridges on both trips for the legend to be a mere hoax. The more likely explanation is that something about the road causes the discrepancy. Perhaps the overhanging limbs of the trees or the foliage blocks the view from the road on the way back. It wouldn't be surprising. The vegetation in that area is thick—so thick, in fact, that at times the road seems to pass into a tunnel of impenetrable green vines. Even when the foliage is not that overgrown, the dirt road itself is always winding. Maybe the curve of the road obscures the vision of the passersby. But while one of these possibilities might be the most likely explanation, some people claim that something more sinister is at work. According to this theory, whether one can count all thirteen bridges is a matter of fate. If the person on the road counts all thirteen bridges, then he will have good luck all the days of his life. But if he counts only twelve bridges, he is doomed. He will be cursed with bad luck, and death may be following close on his heels. A scary proposition, particularly given that stories of drivers counting all thirteen bridges are few and far between.

Some speculate that the ground of Maxwell's Crossing is cursed by activities that occurred during the darker days of the segregation era. Supposedly, during the height of its power in the region, the Ku Klux Klan would often hold rallies just off the crossing. In the wide-open fields nearby, the Klan was said to conduct cross burnings as part of its meetings and initiations. The cross burnings, if they ever really happened, ended many years ago, though some have claimed that the glow of burning fires sometimes glimmers across the field, though no rational cause for the apparent flames is ever discovered.

Whatever the truth may be of the Klan rallies that supposedly happened at Maxwell's Crossing all those years ago, those who visit the open fields around the area report strange and unexplained phenomena to this day. The most frightening of these occurrences involves the spirit of a slave. It is said that at the time of slavery, the man who now haunts the fields escaped from his owners and the plantation on which he was held. Knowing that he could not successfully escape to the North, he decided to take out his years of slavery and frustration on the surrounding countryside.

It is said that he decided to strike where it would hurt the slaveholding plantation owners the most—their children. He went on a rampage, capturing children and teenagers and taking them into the woods, where he would torture and kill them in the most sadistic ways imaginable. This rampage continued for weeks until finally he was hunted down by a posse of men somewhere just off the dirt road that constitutes Maxwell's Crossing today. When he was found, the men didn't bother with a trial. They did not need one to know the man must die. How they carried out the deed is debated to this day. Some say that he was hanged from one of the ancient tall, gnarled trees that grow along the road to this day. Others say that he was taken to a nearby grain silo, where one of the farmers who had lost a daughter to the man's rampage personally beheaded him. Then they dragged his body into the wilderness and threw it into an open pit to be eaten by the birds of the air and beasts of the forest. Of course, some argue that the posse caught the wrong man, and that in the end they executed an innocent. Whatever the truth of the case may be, the children and old-timers around Maxwell's Crossing will tell you that while the men meant to end the horror that had plagued them, their actions served only to give it spiritual permanence.

It is said that to this very day, the spirit of the escaped slave haunts the dirt road of Maxwell's Crossing and the fields that surround it, forever seeking revenge for his execution. Those who have seen him—and lived to tell the tale—say that he is an enormous being, seven feet tall if he is a foot. It is said that he hunts the young people who decide to drive down the road of the thirteen bridges, lying in wait for any who choose to pull to the side for a few moments of forbidden pleasure. Those brave enough—or foolish enough— to do so may find their romantic tryst interrupted in the most violent of ways. The vengeful spirit of the murdered slave will kill anyone he can get his hands on, while stealing their cars and sinking them in the deep river that runs through the area. In fact, some say that you need not even stop to have the killer strike against you. Supposedly, if you even slow down when driving through Maxwell's Crossing, the spirit will hitch a ride and strike you down before you even know what hit you.

How many kids have been killed on the Maxwell's Crossing road? Well, that's a little bit more difficult to ascertain. Everyone knows somebody whose brother or sister or first cousin knows someone else who knew somebody from school who went out on the thirteen bridges road and never came back. Facts any harder than that are hard to come by.

Another legend revolves around strange lights that many people have said they've seen along the road on particularly dark and moonless nights. The legend goes that one will see a light when driving down the road. If the light is green, everything is fine. If the light is red, the person will never be seen again. It's a strange story, but in reality, it has some legitimacy. There is a train trestle near the road that many people use to cross the river on foot. On that trestle is a train signal light. When the light is red, it means a train is coming, and anyone on the bridge might very well be doomed.

Other bizarre occurrences near Maxwell's Crossing involve cars and equipment. Electronic equipment rarely works on Maxwell's Crossing. In fact, full batteries are known to drain away to nothing. Cars break down all the time, an especially frightening occurrence given the sinister stories that hang about the area. Even handbrakes don't work, with parked cars simply rolling backward, even when the car is in park and the brake engaged. These bizarre occurrences often coincide with paranormal events and even the occasional UFO citing. Strange lights in the skies over Maxwell's Crossing are not unusual, though what would draw visitors from outer space to such a place is entirely unclear.

Perhaps the most disturbing story about Maxwell's Crossing involves the sound of a crying baby and the disembodied spirit of a sobbing woman that is said to walk the road at night, searching for the source of the child's cries. The story seems to have originated in the earliest days of the crossing. It is said that the Maxwells were a wealthy family who owned several hundred acres in the area more than a century ago. The family home, a mansion that eventually fell into disrepair, stood along the dirt road that ran along the banks of the Black Warrior River.

Legend has it that one of the servants who worked at the mansion was upset by his treatment at the hands of the Maxwell family. He decided to take out his frustrations on one of the daughters of the Maxwells. She fled from the man, taking her baby and one of the family's carriages to escape. But when she reached the railroad crossing, her carriage became stuck on the railroad tracks. Before she could escape, a train came along and struck the carriage, killing her and her baby. It was from that tragedy that Maxwell's Crossing got its name.

To this day, they say that on nights when the wind is low and the moon is high, you can hear the sound of a baby crying. And if you look closely, you will see the image of a young girl walking along the road near the railroad tracks, still searching for her baby.

The stories from Maxwell's Crossing are all fading into the past, unfortunately. A subdivision was built nearby in recent years, and a gate has been placed over the entrance to the thirteen bridges road. But in the end, maybe it's just as well. The land has always been haunted, and not just by spirits. It is as if the land itself is cursed.

BRYCE HOSPITAL ON THE UNIVERSITY OF ALABAMA CAMPUS

While the University of Alabama is no doubt a historical institution, one that we will discuss in detail shortly, there is another complex near the campus that is, in many ways, even more significant. Originally named the Alabama State Hospital for the Insane, Bryce Hospital is Alabama's oldest and largest psychiatric facility. Opened in 1861, Bryce was a landmark institution, and at the time of its construction, it was a truly state-of-the-art facility.

In spite of its importance—or maybe because of it—the hospital faced mortal danger almost as soon as the doors were opened. When Croxton's raiders came to Tuscaloosa, they considered burning the facility to the ground as a valuable military target. After the administration invited the soldiers inside the building, however, they feared a trap. Deciding that discretion was the better part of valor, the raiders left Bryce unburned, moving on to other targets.

The Alabama State Hospital for the Insane continued on, treating patients with mental illnesses from around the state and the South. Soon, however, the name of the facility was changed to Bryce Hospital in honor of Dr. Peter Bryce, a twenty-seven-year-old pioneer in the field of psychiatrics from South Carolina who became the hospital's first superintendent. Today, the main facility is on the National Register of Historic Places, added in April 1977.

The Italianate building is considered a quintessential example of the architectural model for mental facilities at the time. The hospital was designed based on a popular nineteenth-century concept in the field of psychology known as "moral architecture." Developed by Thomas Story Kirkbride, this principle theorized that beautiful surroundings and uplifting architecture would go far in solving the mental instability of the patients. We see the results of this theory across the country in virtually every mental institution built during the period. It is because of that practice that so many mental institutions are in such impressive structures.

The fatal problem with the Kirkbride theory was twofold. First, as we now know, mental illness is far more complex and occurs for more varied reasons than was believed at the time. Simply put, mental illness requires more sophisticated treatment than a mere change in scenery. In the end, however, it was the second systemic problem that has led to the abandonment of so many Kirkbride facilities—it is simply too expensive to maintain such palatial residences, particularly when they begin to require extensive renovations.

Unfortunately, over time, funding problems became endemic at Bryce Hospital, much as they were throughout the mental facilities of the nation. It was not always so. In the early years of the Alabama State Hospital for the Insane, the hospital was known as a model for the developing science of psychology. Around the world, the general state of mental institutions in the 1800s was often frightfully lacking. But under the direction of Dr. Bryce, the use of shackles, straitjackets and other restraints was severely restricted. The hospital decided to abandon their use altogether in 1882.

Bryce Hospital.

Many of Dr. Bryce's innovations were remarkably forward thinking. At that the time, many practitioners in the field based their treatments on some combination of long-held tradition and pure speculation. Dr. Bryce tried to apply a more regimented treatment plan. His application of an actual scientific method in the place of the more esoteric practices of the day made the hospital a nationally recognized model of the modern treatment for mental disorders.

But by the middle of the twentieth century, conditions at Bryce Hospital had become truly woeful. In 1970, the state of Alabama ranked dead last among U.S. states when it came to funding for mental health treatment. That year, funding was cut even more, despite the fact that 5,200 patients were living at the hospital in filthy conditions that some newspapers compared to those in Nazi concentration camps. Because of these deficiencies, a fifteen-year-old patient named Ricky Wyatt filed what would become one of the largest lawsuits in American history. The lawsuit lasted for thirty-three years and through nine Alabama governors, fourteen state mental commissioners and $15 million in litigation expenses. Still, on the basis of this lawsuit, the federal court system took control of the Alabama healthcare system, imposing minimum standards that have come to be known as the Wyatt Standards. These criteria now serve as a model for the nation.

The days of Bryce Hospital as a mental institution are now limited. In 2009, the University of Alabama reached an agreement with the state government to purchase the Bryce campus in order to expand the college's facilities. The patients who still reside in Bryce will be relocated to another hospital in Tuscaloosa. The Bryce Hospital's main building will remain a historical landmark that will be put to new purpose as a University of Alabama facility. If the paranormal stories of Bryce Hospital are to be believed, however, it seems that the addition of the building to the university will only serve to enhance the haunted reputation of the school.

What sorts of spirits haunt the halls of Bryce Hospital? Even given Dr. Bryce's insistence on humane and modern treatments for the hospital's patients, it cannot be doubted that those who were housed within its walls suffered greatly from the ravages of mental illness. There are also rumors of murders that happened among the patients at Bryce. Many speculate that such suffering somehow results in supernatural and paranormal manifestations. Whatever the case may be, Bryce Hospital is known by many locals as the most haunted location in all of Alabama.

Those who have worked at Bryce are universal in their assertion that strange and supernatural occurrences are almost commonplace there.

Despite the size of the complex, only the main building is still used. Many of the other facilities are unsafe and forbidden to everyone, including employees. The prospect of locked and deserted corridors only adds to the sense of foreboding. But if the stories of visitors and employees alike are to be believed, there is nowhere in Bryce Hospital that is truly empty.

Employees report an eerie feeling that they are never truly alone, and the sensation of being constantly observed is simply one that any new hire must put aside. Even on the very hottest days, the hallways are filled with cold spots. In portions of the hospital that are empty, footsteps echo up and down the hallways. Perhaps most disturbing of all, however, are the voices. Nurses, patients and administrators—they all have heard them. They come in the form of whispers, sometimes soothing, sometimes frightfully violent and filled with rage and hate. They are the voices of the dead, lost souls who came to Bryce Hospital seeking treatment for illnesses that could not be cured, no matter how diligent and caring the staff might be.

The Bryce campus and the buildings that compose it are steeped in history. Much of it represents the steady progress of the science of the mind, including developments that have allowed many people to live ordinary lives that heretofore they could not have imagined. But still, the horrors that its halls have seen from the broken minds of men, women and even children cannot be overstated. If it is true that trauma and tragedy create the perfect conditions for paranormal activity to manifest, then there is no question that Bryce Hospital is filled with the spirits of the dead.

PART II
THE UNIVERSITY OF ALABAMA

Opened in 1831, the roots of the University of Alabama run back to 1818, when Congress authorized the Territory of Alabama to establish a "seminary of learning." On December 18, 1820, the legislature established the University of the State of Alabama just outside Tuscaloosa, the capital of the state at the time.

Famed architect William Nichols was chosen to design the campus, and his plans were heavily influenced by Thomas Jefferson's plan for the University of Virginia. A great rotunda containing the university's library was built in the center of the design, and the campus radiated out from that structure forming the rest of campus.

The University of Alabama thrived in the period before the Civil War, and by 1861, the library was one of the largest in the country. But on the eve of the war, the university was transformed into a military school. It was a fateful decision. Using the university's military function as an excuse, raiding Union soldiers burned the campus to the ground on April 4, 1865, destroying all but four buildings, including the school's library and rotunda.

Reopening in 1871, the university benefited from a large donation of land from Congress in payment for the unfortunate destruction of the campus. No longer a military academy, the school was opened to women in 1892 at the behest of famed education activist Julia Strudwick Tutwiler. That same year, a graduate student named W.G. Little, who had spent time at Harvard University, brought a new sport to the university. That year, the undergraduates at Alabama played their first game of football. Little brought his uniform with him, and since Harvard had been crimson, the football team adopted the same colors, later earning the name the Crimson Tide.

In the early twentieth century, the University of Alabama Crimson Tide established itself as a national powerhouse in the sport of football. That reputation was cemented with a 1925 victory in the historic Rose Bowl game in Los Angeles, California, to secure the school's first national championship. Many more would follow, and Alabama's football success would inspire a devotion to the sport throughout the South that has not waned to this day.

In the 1960s, the University of Alabama was famous for less flattering reasons. While the school was quite progressive when it came to the education of women, the vestiges of slavery and racism were more difficult to shake. Autherine Lucy was the first African American student to successfully enroll at the University of Alabama in 1956, though she was expelled three days later on the basis that the school could not protect her from violence. It was an ironic and inauspicious beginning to the school's efforts to integrate.

In 1963, George Wallace made his infamous and unsuccessful Stand in the Schoolhouse Door at Foster Auditorium, the building that housed registration for the university at the time. His effort was an utterly futile and largely symbolic political stunt, one that ostensibly was meant to be an attempt to prevent the enrollment of African American students Vivian Malone and James Hood into the university. George Wallace knew too well that Attorney General Robert F. Kennedy had sent his deputy, Nicholas Katzenbach, along with a veritable army of federal marshals, to escort the two students and ensure that they succeeded in their enrollment efforts. Malone would become the first African American student to graduate from the University of Alabama, though both Lucy and Hood would eventually graduate as well. The university has come a long way from those dark days. In 2010, the plaza in front of the Foster Auditorium was rededicated the Malone-Hood Plaza, with the Autherine Lucy Clock Tower built in the center of the plaza.

Today, the University of Alabama covers some two thousand acres and holds nearly three hundred buildings. In addition to enrolling thirty thousand students on its main campus, the university also maintains satellite campuses in Huntsville and Birmingham.

Over the 180 years of its history, the University of Alabama has seen much in the way of change and development. From a frontier college, to a Civil War military school, to symbol of racial integration, to a nationally recognized institute of learning and a college football powerhouse, many souls have passed through its doors. If some stories are to be believed, not all of these souls have left.

THE KILGORE HOUSE

Every day, hundreds of University of Alabama students pass a lovely blue and white Queen Anne house just off one of the school's main thoroughfares. Most of them never notice it. There is something about the house, the way it seems to blend in to its surroundings, even though it is in many ways completely out of place. Perhaps it is a defensive reaction. Maybe those who wander the campus—especially at night—would rather not notice the ordinary-looking house in the midst of campus. Mystery surrounds the old house, and while we know much of its official history, it is what remains shrouded in rumor and speculation that is most intriguing.

Known as the Kilgore House, the building was constructed in 1890. The trustees of the Alabama Hospital for the Insane—now known as Bryce Mental Institution—decided that their assistant steward and chief engineer, Charles C. Kilgore, deserved a "commodious two-story cottage" in which he and his family would live. Captain Kilgore—a nickname he earned fighting as a fifteen-year-old boy in the Civil War—was a dedicated servant to the hospital, working in various capacities since shortly after the end of the conflict. These jobs included overseeing the outdoor activities of the hospital and its patients such as agriculture, mining and construction.

The location chosen for the Kilgore House was rather unusual. It was more or less built in the midst of a burying plot. It is unclear whether the house sat on any graves, but if one looked out the front windows, the view would have been of the university cemetery.

Despite the unsavory location, Kilgore needed the accommodations. In addition to his seven children, he also took care of his niece, Cora Kilgore. Cora went to the Tuscaloosa Women's College with Kilgore's youngest daughter, Gibbie Kilgore. Sadly, Gibbie succumbed to dysentery in the summer of 1901, when she was only sixteen.

In 1904, Cora started graduate studies at the University of Alabama. The Kilgores, having an empty house now that the children were grown, decided to open their home to Alabama co-eds. The young women who were lucky enough to live in the Kilgore House were greatly envied by the other girls on campus. Although nominally supervised by the first female faculty member at the University of Alabama (she also lived in what was then called the Kilgore Ranch), the girls ran wild, hosting parties that featured dancing and other scandalous behavior. Other girls on campus were said to take an oath: "Covet not thy Kilgore neighbor's eatings, nor their dancing, nor their suitors, nor their walks, nor anything that is not thine own."

The Kilgore House.

But there was a darker side to the Kilgore Ranch. It was an age when a belief in mysticism was on the rise, when people moved in the shadows, seeking to speak and commune with the dead. At night, the Kilgore girls were said to tell one another's fortunes and even engage in séances. It is unknown how successful they were in their efforts. Nor was Cora's mysterious death in 1908 at the tender age of twenty ever explained. All we can say for sure is that the Kilgores no longer opened their home to campus co-eds after her tragic passing, abandoning the home to other Bryce Hospital employees soon thereafter. But if the *Alabama Heritage* magazine employees whose offices now occupy the house are to be believed, something else stayed behind.

For many years, the house sat silent. There were no tales of the spirits that might haunt it, no stories of late night visitors or unexplained apparitions. But then, in September 2008, one hundred years after Cora's passing and the night after the biggest full moon anyone could remember, the house that had been dead came alive.

During a single day and night in October, three different employees bore witness to paranormal phenomena they could not explain. One worker felt the bitterest cold she had ever experienced and heard noises that disturbed her so deeply that she fled the house. Another heard footsteps when she knew she was alone. Most shocking and unexplainable of all, a longtime volunteer witnessed the apparition of an African American woman in a turban and work dress walking through the lower levels of the house. A single such occurrence would be hard to explain. The woman saw the same apparition eight times in the span of four hours.

Now, paranormal activity seems to occur in the house with regular frequency. Volunteers, employees and visitors report constantly feeling as though they are being watched even when no one is in the house. They hear the sound of furniture moving. Equipment turns on when it isn't plugged in or turns off in the middle of use. Doors slam on their own. The chandelier is known to move whenever someone walks above it. Many times, the chandelier will start swinging even when the upstairs floor is empty. Batteries drain away, wireless technology will not work at all and even plugged-in cameras will not function.

Whispered words seem constantly to float through the halls of the Kilgore House. The younger people and students who have worked at the house repeatedly report hearing a conversation between a man and a woman, but one not clear enough to make out. There is the sound of a child singing, usually very early in the morning when the house is still and quiet. It is a sweet voice, a soothing song, but nothing that can be explained as part of the physical world as we know it.

One employee reports seeing what she can only describe as a black "thing" that moves so quickly through the room that she can never make it out clearly, but not so fast that it could be anything other than a figure. Sometimes she feels it watching her throughout the day, only to see a flash of blackness disappear whenever she turns. Another spirit has the ability to mimic voices. The employees report hearing co-workers call their names or tell them hello only to discover that they are alone.

All of this activity has prompted the employees of the Kilgore House to attempt to record evidence of their encounters. Their tape recorders have revealed men, women, children, babies and even dogs. The name Zula once came up on tape. An unusual name, to be sure, but graduate students at the University of Alabama discovered that a Zula once lived at the house. The resemblance between Zula and the woman who caught the name on tape was uncanny.

Some of the activity revolves around a sword of Captain Kilgore's that remains in the house. The sword is a decorative item of the Freemasons. The sword has been moved from room to room, and wherever the sword resides,

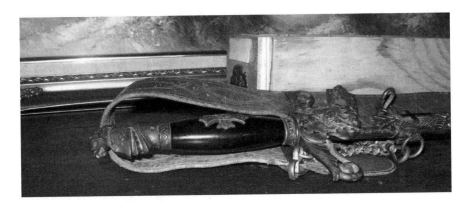

The haunted sword.

the black figure appears. Some have speculated that while Captain Kilgore may not have died in the house, he returned there nevertheless, perhaps to reclaim the sword that has his name engraved on it.

Yes, the Kilgore House is both mysterious and innocuous. If you wish to visit, you will have to make an effort to find it. But some places are better left alone.

THE LITTLE ROUND HOUSE

It is hard to imagine today what it must have been like in those dark days in April 1865. Four years earlier, things had been very different on the campus of the University of Alabama and across the South. For decades, the fissures between the Southern states and their Northern brethren had grown increasingly unsalvageable with every passing year. Rooted in the question of slavery, Northern and Southern politicians formed political blocs based more on regional loyalty than the type of issue-based disagreements we experience today. In Congress, power was divided between slave states and non-slave states, with the Southern bloc garnering extra representation in the House of Representatives due to its slave population. The uneasy truce between the blocs could only have lasted as long as the equilibrium was maintained. But the United States was a country on the move, and westward expansion would almost destroy it.

With the victory of the United States over Mexico in 1848 and the Gadsden Purchase of 1853, the nation gained huge swaths of territory for settlement. The settlers came, driven by the belief in Manifest Destiny that was widespread at the time. Soon, states were ready to be admitted to the Union, and the question had to be answered—would they be free or slave?

The addition of a free state without a slave state to counterbalance it would lead to a shift in power in Congress. The Civil War didn't start until the election of Abraham Lincoln, but the breakup began much earlier. Decades before and leading up to secession, the territories were engaged in bloody internecine warfare, struggles to determine which side—slave or free—the states would join upon their entry into the nation. Men such as John Brown led paramilitary actions that produced monikers like Bleeding Kansas. With bands of marauders killing one another and John Brown's execution after an assault on Harpers Ferry intended to spur a slave revolt, things had reached a breaking point. Many people in states both north and south of the Mason-Dixon line were simply looking for an excuse to separate. The election of Abraham Lincoln in 1860 gave them that excuse. Alabama helped lead the way.

Politics in 1860 were dominated in Alabama by the so-called Fire Eaters, led by William Lowndes Yancey. Yancey helped split the Democratic Party in two, leading a walkout of the Alabama contingent of the party's convention in Charleston. Many of the other Southern delegations went with him, and a divided Democratic Party could never contend with the newly minted Republicans and their Free-Soil platform. But Abraham Lincoln did not carry a single slaveholding state. In fact, in the fifteen states that allowed slavery, Lincoln won just 2 counties out of 996, both in Missouri. In Alabama, no ballots were cast for Lincoln.

South Carolina was the first state to issue an article of secession. Alabama followed close behind. Despite some pockets of unionist support, there was jubilation throughout the state when independence was announced and the Confederacy born, with Montgomery as its first capital.

At first, the South won battle after battle as superior leadership overcame deficits in manpower and war materiel. Names like Manassas and Chancellorsville gave the Southern partisans hope that perhaps they could defeat the North after all. In time, however, a combination of the vast advantages held by the Union, as well as the emergence of generals like Tecumseh Sherman and Ulysses S. Grant, turned the tide for the North. Four years later, the initial jubilation Southerners had felt turned to bitter sorrow and devastation.

By April 1865, the war was all but over. Over one million men had been killed or wounded, and much of the South was burning to the ground. On

April 3, on the same day that Richmond fell to the army of Ulysses S. Grant, Union soldiers began to converge on the University of Alabama campus. It was on that day that the legend of a building just off the quad, the Little Round House, was born.

The Little Round House was built as a guardhouse in the days that the University of Alabama served as a military institution. The university's third president, Landon Cabell Garland, took pity on the young students who were forced to keep watch every night, even in the wind and rain. The Little Round House provided excellent protection. It also served as the headquarters for the university drum corps.

We can only imagine what it was like on that April day when the drum corps—drilled relentlessly for four years—was finally called into action. There had been rumors for weeks that Union soldiers were skulking about the outskirts of Tuscaloosa. News was sparse back in those days, and with communication lines cut all across the state and the South, rumor and innuendo were the truth of the day. Unfortunately for the cadets and the university they protected, when the Union soldiers came, there was no need to speculate about their presence. They came in force, and they came with destruction on their minds.

The Little Round House.

On Monday, April 3, the cadets at the University of Alabama followed their daily routine. They awoke early, assembling on the parade grounds at six o'clock that morning for review. They could not know that Brigadier General John T. Croxton and his 1,500 raiders were advancing steadily toward Northport and the bridge that passed over the Black Warrior River. The Union soldiers took the bridge after only a brief skirmish, killing one of the Rebel defenders in the process.

That evening it was, as all such nights must be, dark and stormy. The Union soldiers advanced under the cover of nightfall, encircling the town and the university. It was nigh on midnight when a rider from town came flying up the road to the President's Mansion. Following a brief conversation, it was President Garland himself who ran across the campus to the Round House, screaming for the boys to beat the long roll on the drum, the universal military signal to assemble. The young men, no more than boys really, dressed quickly and assembled with their gear and their guns to receive their orders.

Through the misty rain the boys advanced into town, but it was not long before they came upon Union skirmishers. A firefight broke out, but the well-trained cadets won the moment, forcing the Federal skirmishers into retreat. Unfortunately, it would be a short-lived triumph.

The cadets settled in on top of a prominence known as River Hill. Battle was joined, but it quickly became clear that the cadets were in an impossible situation. They were outnumbered five to one by seasoned veterans of many Civil War battles. To make matters worse, the cavalrymen carried the newest technology, rifles known as "repeaters." Unlike the cadets' muskets, which required a lengthy reloading process between each shot, the repeaters fired cartridges and could shoot multiple times before reloading was necessary.

It was President Garland who made the fateful decision. Fighting was suicidal. Even if the boys held off the Union soldiers for a little while, this was no Alamo. Reinforcements were not coming, and there was no victory to be had. Garland gave the order to retreat. The cadets fled reluctantly back to the university, filling their bags with as much as they could carry in supplies and ammunition before retreating out of town.

The Union soldiers acted quickly. With nothing to stop them, they burned to the ground the University of Alabama, including its library and its iconic rotunda. They also set fire to the local cotton mill and supply stores, as well as several factories in town. From their defensive, elevated position several miles away, the cadets could see the smoke of their beloved university as it was put to the flame.

It was a bitter and unavoidable tragedy, one of the last of the war. Only one day later, General Grant issued orders throughout the army to cease the scorched earth and total war tactics the Union had previously employed and focus only on Rebel armies. Then, on April 9, a mere five days after the university was put to the torch, General Robert E. Lee surrendered the Army of Northern Virginia at Appomattox Court House. The war, for all practical purposes, was over.

But all of it came too late to save the University of Alabama and the generations of students who suffered because of the setback inflicted by its destruction. Yet while much of the school was gone, the Little Round House, one of the few buildings on campus that actually served a military purpose, survived. Some say something else survived with it.

Today, the Little Round House is commonly known as the Jasons' Shrine, having earned that name because of its connection with university honors societies and, in particular, the secret society known as the Jasons. One does not tarry long around the Little Round House, however, without detecting a distinctive feeling of unease and foreboding. Some say there is a reason for such unease.

The stories surrounding the Little Round House are impossible to prove and may, in fact, be utterly fictitious. One story says that two of the cadets decided not to follow orders when instructed to abandon the university. Instead, they stayed behind, intent on enacting their own brand of justice and revenge on any Federal soldiers they could find.

The boys were clever and designed a ruse. One remained outside, waiting until a group of Yankee soldiers found him. The soldiers asked the boy where they could find some whiskey, a question any good Confederate could expect from the degenerate and godless Yankees. The boy led the three soldiers to the Little Round House, where his companion waited inside, pistol cocked and ready. When the three men entered, the young Rebel cadet fired on the unsuspecting men, killing them all. The two boys then escaped north, rejoining their regiment and escaping whatever Yankee justice was due them.

People say that if you go to the Little Round House at night and put your ear to the door, you can still hear the sound of the three men rummaging about for the whiskey long ago promised them. Others say that the spirits of three men in Union blue can be seen wandering the campus at night, specifically in the vicinity of the Little Round House, forever condemned to search for the boys who murdered them. It is a search that goes on in vain.

The stench of murder must surround the Little Round House, for there is a second story about a ghost that haunts it, another young man said to have been killed unjustly by Confederate soldiers. It is told that prior to the burning of the University of Alabama, a soldier was dispatched by Croxton, under a flag of truce, to parlay with the Rebels who controlled the campus grounds. The cadets, it is said, had made it known that they were interested in surrendering to avoid bloodshed. But their intentions were far more devious. When the unsuspecting soldier arrived on campus, he was captured and taken to the Little Round House. There he was beaten and tortured, all the frustrations of four years of unsuccessful war piled on top of him, before the Rebels finally murdered him in cold blood. According to this story, Croxton's merciless destruction of the campus was due in no small part to his rage at learning of this horrid violation of the laws of war. But the spirit of the soldier was not so easily appeased. It is said that on moonless nights, you can see his spectral form wandering about the campus, specifically in the vicinity of the Little Round House, his moaning sobs crying out for justice.

Whatever the truth of these stories—and there is little in the historical record to support them—the fact of the matter is that the Little Round House is, in many ways, a shunned structure. More than a few faculty members or students have reported witnessing spectral phenomena in the vicinity of the Little Round House. Whether the ghost of long-dead Union soldiers or the spirits of someone else whose story is lost to time, it appears something other than history haunts the small round building on the quad of the University of Alabama.

THE QUAD

Located at in the middle of the University of Alabama is a great space of open ground known as the quadrangle or, more commonly, the quad. The quad is both the spiritual, historical and physical heart of the Alabama campus. About twenty-two acres, the quad was home to most of the University of Alabama's original buildings. Much like the historic rotunda that once stood on its edge, the quad itself was patterned after Thomas Jefferson's plan for the University of Virginia. The quad was designed as a large expanse of open space with trees on one side for studying and grassy fields on the other for play.

The quad's central location continued even after the original campus was burned during the Civil War. The oldest and most historic buildings on campus are still located on the quad, including the Gorgas House, Toumey

The Quad, Denny Chimes.

Hall, Oliver Barnard Hall and the Little Round House. In addition to those structures, the Amelia Gayle Gorgas Library and Denny Chimes also rise from the quad.

The ceremonial Mound, site of the old Franklin Hall, is constructed from the remains of the original buildings that were burned by Union troops. Following that destruction, what was left of the structures was piled up and buried. Whether intentionally or by accident, that pile of burned remains became a symbolic meeting place on campus. It can an also be found in the confines of the quad.

The Mound is not the only place on the quad where the past of the university is buried. Also beneath the quad are the ruins of several dorm buildings that were burned, as well as the charred remnants of the original library and its thousands of books, all lost at the hands of the last days of the Civil War.

The destruction of the university was the result of a decision by the Alabama legislature to convert the college into a military system shortly before the beginning of the Civil War. The university produced a large number of highly qualified officers during that time, earning the moniker "the West Point of the Confederacy." That honor would prove disastrous in the spring of 1865, when Union brigadier general John T. Croxton and his 1,500 cavalrymen captured Tuscaloosa on April 4. Two hundred of these men were sent to the university with orders to burn it to the ground, led by Colonel Thomas M. Johnston. The faculty pleaded with Johnston to spare the library, one of the largest in the country at that time, and the historic rotunda. Johnston, who considered himself a scholar, agreed that such destruction would be as wasteful as it would be tragic. He sent a courier to General Croxton, requesting permission to spare the library. Croxton, however, was in no mood for mercy. His orders were clear, and he conveyed to Johnston his command to burn to the ground all public buildings, including the library.

Then something truly remarkable happened. It's not clear who it was that did it. Perhaps it was Johnston himself. Maybe it was one of his aides. It could have been Andre Deloffre, the university's librarian. But whoever the person, someone present at the burning of the university library that day entered the building before it was put to the flame and took one book—just one tome that was to be the only book to survive the destruction. How they chose the book is as great a mystery as who it was who did the choosing. It will no doubt remain a mystery for all time. But upon leaving the rotunda, one of the men present carried with him a translation published in 1853 entitled *The Koran: Commonly Called the Alcoran of Mohammed*. The book sits in the university's W.S. Hoole Special Collections Library, a testament to the advanced nature of the school at the time and all that was lost in the flames of the Civil War.

Those flames consumed the University of Alabama that day, 150 years ago. The rotunda housing the library was thus put to the torch, and by the time Johnston was finished, only seven buildings remained, the last vestiges of what the University of Alabama had originally been.

As noted earlier, many of the ruins were buried, while the bricks of the destroyed structures were used to build the first new structures on campus. The first of these buildings was Woods Hall, completed in 1868 just north of the quad. Originally containing a dorm for military cadets, a dining hall and classrooms, Woods Hall is now the center of the University's Department of Art and Art History, a place of creative thinking that emerged from one of the country's most destructive wars.

But the vast majority of the quad is simply made up of empty space. Many of the largest campus gatherings occur there. Every Saturday in the fall, thousands of Alabamians—alumni, students and simple fans of the school—gather there to tailgate before Alabama Crimson Tide football games. The quad is also home to pep rallies the Friday before games and a large bonfire and concert the week of Homecoming, as well as untold numbers of official and unofficial gatherings of students and visitors.

In fact, the quad was the first on-campus site of Alabama Crimson Tide football games. While it may be difficult to imagine, a sport now watched by over a 100,000 spectators was originally played on the grass of the quad. That tradition carried on for twenty-one years before games were moved to Denny Field, the site of today's Bryant-Denny Stadium.

The quad survived the flurry of construction that followed the University of Alabama's rapid growth during the twentieth century. The quad is now surrounded by buildings of every type, specialty and size, making it the center of academic life at the school.

During the day, the quad has a reputation as a welcoming place where students can play a game of touch football or have a picnic with friends. But at night, the atmosphere dramatically changes. Maybe it's the fact that the open spaces do not lend themselves to artificial lighting. Maybe it's the fog that seems to gather preternaturally during the dark watches of the night. Or maybe something else walks unseen among the trees of the University of Alabama's most expansive natural treasure. Whatever the case may be, many students and faculty have reported experiencing strange—and unexplained—phenomena when the moon is full and the night at its darkest.

Like so much on the university campus, the stories of ghostly encounters on the quad often seem to revolve around things that happened during the Civil War. At least four different Civil War soldiers are said to haunt the quad, though whether they are Union or Confederate is open for debate. One popular tale focuses on what has been described as an exceptionally tall man in a Confederate military uniform. The man roams the grounds of the quad when the night is foggy or even on some days that are dry and dusty. The man is said to be flanked by two other individuals, though their particular description is never as detailed as his. The general view held by those who know of the story is that the tall man is the former commandant of the cadets himself, while the two men are former faculty members whose bodies were cremated after their deaths and their ashes scattered across the quad.

Another popular story focuses on a man of unknown history who many claim walks across the quad on clear nights beneath the stars. It is said that he committed suicide a century ago, hanging himself from one of the trees that stands to this day on the campus.

The wide-open spaces of the quad were perfect for military drills and parades during its days as a military institution. The University of Alabama ceased to be such a military institution over one hundred years ago, but according to some witnesses, the old drills never quite ended. On particularly dark and foggy nights, it is said that the sound of the long roll of a drum echoes across the open quad, arousing long-dead cadets to assemble in preparation for the day Union troops might arrive on campus. As we've mentioned before, in April 1865, that day came.

On that day, the young students assembled on the quad, where they marched out to meet the advancing Union cavalrymen. In the end, their efforts were little more than symbolic. After firing a few volleys from their rifles, the students retreated, and none was killed. But they must have felt a pang of guilt and bitterness as they watched their beloved university burn to the ground. Perhaps some of them felt they should have done more. Maybe one or two wanted to go back and fight, even as their more level-headed companions convinced them that they didn't stand a chance. Whatever might have happened in those days long ago, it is apparent that many of the long-dead cadets do not rest easy. When the long roll sounds in the dead of night and the smell of smoke and burning buildings wafts through the trees, perhaps it is the restless spirits of those young soldiers begging for one last chance to save the school they so loved.

The stories of haunted happenings extend to Oliver Bernard and Toumey Halls, two of the oldest buildings on campus. At night, students have reported having a particularly uneasy feeling when inside these two old structures. The stairs squeak constantly, as if people are walking up and down them. The elevators behave in bizarre ways, the door suddenly opening or the cars moving up and down between floors when no living soul is present. Even on the hottest nights, cold spots seem to float around the rooms, sucking both the heat and the calm from whatever student they touch. Some students and faculty have sworn never to enter the two buildings at night if they are alone.

The quad is the heart of the college's campus, and it is certainly naturally beautiful. But it has seen some of the darkest days of the University of Alabama, days that could have been the very end of the school itself. If the students and faculty who live and attend classes at the university today are to be believed, there are restless spirits that have not forgotten those days, and they continue to relieve them, even from beyond the grave.

SMITH HALL

Just off the quad at the University of Alabama stands one of the most interesting buildings on the university campus. Smith Hall, named after Dr. Eugene Allen Smith, houses the Alabama Museum of Natural History, the oldest museum in the state. The museum contains everything from artifacts related to geology, zoology, mineralogy, paleontology, ethnology, history and photography to bizarre and interesting bits of Alabama history. For instance, in addition to complete prehistoric animal skeletons, the museum also houses a meteorite that hit a woman in 1954, the only natural space artifact that is known to have ever struck a human being.

Dr. Smith was a renowned scientist. Appointed the state geologist of Alabama in 1873, Dr. Smith spent the next forty years of his life mapping and collecting specimens from around the state. Smith Hall was built in the early 1900s and was formally dedicated in 1910. After Smith's death, his wife, Amelia, took over the directorship of the museum, making her one of the few women to head such an operation in that day and age.

Smith Hall.

Smith Hall was designed to mirror many of the other history museums that began to spring up around the country at the turn of the century, particularly those in Chicago, New York and Washington, D.C. Although built on a smaller scale than its sister museums, Smith Hall remains an impressive structure. The main entrance is framed by a colonnade of eight columns. Upon entering, one is met by a massive central staircase of Alabama marble that leads to the Grand Gallery on the second floor. The central building is three stories tall, with two-story wings sweeping off to either side. The two wings originally housed the Department of Geology and the Department of Biology. While those two departments have since moved to other buildings, the wings still contain classrooms and active laboratories. A barrel-vaulted ceiling provides natural light through a number of skylights.

Perhaps it is the dark hardwood floors, the massive windows, the skeleton of a massive prehistoric whale or the collection of shrunken heads, but something about Smith Hall has turned it into a place with a reputation for the paranormal and the unexplained. Students at the University of Alabama are said to shun the place—many spend their entire careers at the college without ever going near it, much less inside it. Whatever the explanation, something uncanny and unnatural appears to haunt the corridors of Smith Hall.

One of the incidents most often associated with Smith Hall involves the carriage of Dr. Smith himself. Upon his death, the carriage was added as an exhibit on the main floor of the museum. Visitors to the museum claim to have heard the sound of wheels and horses inside the building, as if someone were riding the carriage on a mad dash through its halls.

Others claim to have personally witnessed the sound of footsteps echoing across the marbled steps, even when the building is empty. Perhaps the most enduring story involves one of the upstairs classrooms. Some students have claimed to have heard the sounds of a lecturing professor coming from the rooms above, even in the middle of the night, as if a spectral class is taking place that they cannot see. They have even claimed to have heard the voices of students changing classes, and the elevator in the building is known to move up and down between floors, even when no one—alive, at least—is present. Speculation among those who have been a part of such paranormal occurrences ranges far and wide, but many say they believe that Dr. Smith himself is one of the spirits that haunts the hall. Some young ladies have even claimed to have seen the image of Dr. Smith in the mirror of the women's restroom on the main floor of the building. Dr. Smith's desk is kept upstairs with a display honoring his contributions to the museum. A small red velvet rope separates the desk from the general public. Occasionally,

The haunted buggy at Smith Hall.

when the spirit of Dr. Smith seems to be at its most active, the rope will move of its own accord, swinging back and forth for no apparent reason.

One group of students once followed what they believed was an intruder that had broken into the building late at night. After tracking the sound of footsteps and voices into a classroom, they were startled to find the normally well-ordered desks strewn all about the room, with no sign of the intruder they had been tracking. It was only later that they discovered the truth. According to legend, years before, a boiler explosion had killed a number of students in that very room. Perhaps they have never left.

One of the most disturbing stories involving Smith Hall comes from the basement, where students still work in the labs. Quite often, students who are working late in the laboratory have the feeling that they are being watched by some unseen entity. One assistant who experienced that feeling also thought he heard a noise from one of the laboratory closets. As he looked inside, he was pushed from behind and locked within. Although he tried to free himself, the door would not budge and did not open until morning. Needless to say, the student's desire to investigate the strange occurrences at Smith Hall was somewhat diminished after that experience.

Without question, Smith Hall remains and will always be one of the most magnificent buildings on the University of Alabama campus. But one can't walk through its corridors without feeling a sense of unease. Something moves within Smith Hall, something not quite normal. Perhaps it is the spirit of the building's namesake. Maybe it is the ghost of students killed within its walls decades ago. But whatever it is, you can be certain that you are never alone in Smith Hall. And when you leave, Smith Hall does not sit empty. It is quite possible that it never truly does.

ALLEN BALES THEATRE

Rowand-Johnson Hall was built in 1955 as the home of the University of Alabama's Department of Theater and Dance. It is a rather ordinary campus building, built in the minimalistic style of the time. But while Rowand-Johnson has little to distinguish it from any other classroom building, there is one thing that makes it interesting: Allen Bales Theatre.

Alan Bales was born in Birmingham, but he spent the majority of his life in Tuscaloosa. A graduate of the University of Alabama in 1943, Dr. Bales was a hero in the Second World War, serving in an antiaircraft battalion in Europe. After surviving the war, Dr. Bales returned to

Allen Bales Theatre.

Tuscaloosa, where he earned yet another degree, this time his master's, in 1947. He became a professor of speech that year, serving the university until his retirement in 1982.

But while speech was his specialty, his true love and passion was for theater. Dr. Bales was widely renowned as an actor and lauded for his work as a theater director. During his lifetime, he toured nationally with the Kaleidoscope Players theater company. He received a number of awards, both for his work as an actor and theater director and for his contribution to theater in the state of Alabama. It is no wonder that the University of Alabama chose to name one of the theaters in Rowand-Johnson Hall after him.

Interestingly, though, it is not Allen Bales who is said to haunt the theaters of that building. It is Marian Gallaway, whose spirit is believed to still walk the halls and the aisles of the theaters within. Gallaway was the theater director at the University of Alabama during the mid-twentieth century. While Mrs. Gallaway has been dead for many years, some students in the Theater Department claim that she has never quite left the campus.

It is said that a young actor may summon Mrs. Gallaway if he is so inclined. The student in question need only stand alone on the stage and ask, "How is my blocking, Mrs. Gallaway?" If the student looks up to the projection booth high in the theater above the entrances, he will see Marian Gallaway—or her spectral presence, at least. Students claim that the spirit is unmistakably the old theater director. A great portrait of her hangs in the lobby of the theater, and there are few who pass by it every day who would not recognize Gallaway the instant they saw her or, in this case, summoned her.

But one need not call on Mrs. Gallaway to have her attendance at a show. Rumor has it that she regularly attends performances. Gallaway seems to be particularly fond of Tennessee Williams plays. Tennessee Williams and Gallaway were known to be good friends during the playwright's most productive years. In fact, many claim that the character of Blanche DuBois in *A Street Car Named Desire* is patterned after Gallaway's life. Whatever the truth may be of such wild rumors, more than one cast member or audience attendee has claimed to see Gallaway sitting in the second row, by every appearance enjoying herself quite a bit. What makes these witnesses all the more credible is that they are completely unaware that she is dead, having come to know Gallaway only by the portrait hanging in the entranceway to the theater. Thus, when they see her spirit, they often don't realize that they have had a ghostly encounter. Who knows how many people have come into contact with Mrs. Gallaway, unaware of the significance of their encounter and believing her only to be a kindly old lady, one who must have done something quite grand to earn a painting in the lobby.

In addition to her performance haunts, Mrs. Gallaway has also been seen wandering the stage or hallways of the theater, dressed all in white. She's even been seen outside on occasion on the sidewalk in front of Rowand-Johnson Hall. Other times, students report hearing slamming doors and other loud noises when they are in the theater late at night, usually when they are goofing off instead of learning their lines.

It seems that Mrs. Gallaway loved the theater so much, she never wanted to leave. For her, the show always goes on.

THE GORGAS HOUSE

The University of Alabama has seen 180 years of history, but there is only one structure on the campus that has been there since even before the beginning. It was standing when the university opened, and it saw the campus burn at the hands of marauding Union soldiers. It survived two world wars and the integration of the campus. It stands today as one of the most historic and beautiful structures on the university campus.

Still, perhaps because it sits in a shady part of campus just off the quad, many students have probably never even noticed the home known as the Gorgas House. It's unfortunate, too, because the Gorgas House has a truly remarkable history. There is not a student who has attended the University of Alabama who has not had the Gorgas House preside over his or her passing through the college's halls. It is the one constant at a place that has seen so much change.

The Gorgas House was built in 1829, an example of the Greek Revival style popular in Alabama and much of the South at the time. Two sweeping staircases led up to a colonnaded second-floor entrance to the mostly brick building. The Gorgas House was designed by William Nichols, an English man by birth and the same architect who planned the original campus and the Old Alabama State Capitol. Given that both the old campus and the old capitol were burned to the ground over the last century and a half, the Gorgas House has become Nichols's legacy.

Initially, the Gorgas House was used as a guesthouse for visitors to the university, as well as professors who needed temporary lodging. It then

The Gorgas House.

transitioned into a dining hall for students before being converted into a full-time residence for faculty in the late 1840s.

The Gorgas House earned its name from one of the truly remarkable families in Alabama history—the Gorgas family. It began with Josiah Gorgas, the seventh University of Alabama president and longtime resident of the home. Gorgas was appointed president of the university in 1878 after serving as head of the University of the South in Sewanee, Tennessee. Gorgas had spent time in the Confederate army during the Civil War, attaining the rank of general before becoming chief of ordnance for the entire Confederate military. After ill health as the result of a stroke forced him to resign as president, the trustees of the university decided to give the Gorgas House as a retirement home for Josiah. Following his retirement, the university created the position of librarian for him, in which capacity he served until his death in 1883.

Perhaps the most famous Gorgas, at least in the minds of most Alabama students, is Amelia Gayle Gorgas, the wife of Josiah Gorgas. Amelia was the daughter of John Gayle, governor of Alabama when the university opened its doors. The Gayle family was well respected in both the state and the larger nation, and Amelia Gayle was even present in Washington, D.C., when the cornerstone of the Washington Monument was laid. Amelia married Josiah and, after the war, came with him to the university's rebuilding campus. When Josiah became president of the university, she took the position of hospital matron. She held that position until Josiah's death.

Her relationship with the university did not end with Josiah's passing, however. Instead, she took over his position as librarian, adding the job of postmistress as well in 1886. She held the position of librarian for twenty-three years.

Amelia took her job as librarian very seriously. Rather than just treating her position as librarian as ceremonial, she set out to vastly expand the reach of the library, increasing the number of books it contained from six thousand to twenty thousand volumes. Amelia died in 1913, but her memory has not been forgotten. The university's main library—which sits right next to the Gorgas House—now bears her name. It was the first building on campus to be named after a woman.

Amelia and Josiah had a total of five children. One of them, William Crawford Gorgas, accomplished particular fame. A doctor and surgeon general of the army, William is famous throughout the world as the man who finally defeated the scourge of the mosquito, eradicating yellow fever in both Cuba and South America and going a long way to stopping the spread of malaria. In addition to improving the lives of countless millions, William was tasked by President Theodore Roosevelt himself with protecting workers on the Panama Canal, long hampered by the scourge of the disease. After decades of failure because of the constant threat of yellow fever, the great canal was finally completed due in large part to William's efforts.

In 1944, the Alabama legislature designated the house as a memorial to the Gorgas family for their dedication to the university and the state. The house remained in their family until 1953, when the last resident of the house, Maria Gorgas, passed away. Today, the Gorgas House serves as one of the University of Alabama's museums and honors the legacy of the Gorgas family and all that its members did for the university, the state and the world.

Of course, given the long and storied history of the Gorgas House, it is no surprise that stories of hauntings and the ghostly spirits of the home's occupants remain vivid and widely reported to this day. It is said that after decades of shepherding students through their time at the university, Amelia Gorgas has not allowed death to hamper her work. One story focuses on her habit of sitting on the porch at the Gorgas House well into the night, rocking and greeting passersby. It is said that on many evenings, if the visitor is worthy of the effort, the rocking chairs will move on their own in greeting, as if their long-dead owner were still there, watching.

Josiah Gorgas is also said to haunt his old home. Late at night, when the home is empty of all but the docents who maintain it, the workers occasionally hear the sound of a man walking up the stairs of the house, making a peculiar banging sound as he passes. They say it is old Josiah Gorgas, still wearing the sword of a general of the Confederate army, which bangs against the wall every time he takes a step.

Next to the Gorgas House sits a small pile of dirt known simply as the Mound. The Mound is sacred to the honors and secret societies of the campus and is built from the burned debris of the university buildings destroyed by the Union attack of April 1865. Many years ago, three professors had their ashes spread on the Mound after their deaths so that they would never have to leave the school behind. It is said by some that on particularly windy and cloudless nights when the moon is full, three men can be glimpsed by the

A bedroom in the Gorgas House.

81

careful watcher standing on the Mound. But if the intruder tries to speak to the men, they simply vanish as if they were never there in the first place.

The spirits that haunt the Gorgas House and the surrounding areas are not frightening or threatening. In fact, nothing could be further from the truth. Those who have encountered the spirits of Josiah Gorgas and particularly Amelia Gorgas talk about having a feeling of protection. It seems that in death, Amelia Gorgas continues to watch over students and visitors to the University of Alabama campus, just as she did all the days of her life.

Whether these stories are true or merely fables is open to debate. But one thing we can know for certain: the Gorgas House will remain on campus just as it has always been, a symbol of the past and a repository of the university's history.

AMELIA GAYLE GORGAS LIBRARY

While the quad has its share of stories, there's one building on that grassy expanse that deserves its own special consideration. The Amelia Gayle Gorgas Library is named after the matron of the university. Amelia Gayle Gorgas was beloved by the students, with one writing in the school yearbook, *The Corolla*, that if the only thing he gained from school was his friendship with her, he would consider his time in college well spent. *The Corolla* was dedicated to Amelia a number of times, and few, if any, University of Alabama faculty were ever as loved as she.

After Amelia Gayle Gorgas's death, there was a movement among the students to honor her in some way. Since she had been the school's librarian for twenty-three years, it only made sense to name the library after her. When the new library was constructed on the quad in 1941, it was named after Amelia Gayle Gorgas.

Five stories tall, the library contains over one million books, as well as state-of-the-art computer technology, classrooms, a study area and even a coffee shop. While not the only library on campus, Amelia Gayle Gorgas is the main library and, for many students, the center of campus intellectual life. In many ways, the library is no different from any number of similar buildings on any other college grounds. But there are certain students who claim that the halls of Gorgas Library are never empty, no matter what the hour. And it's not because some students study at all hours of the night. They say that Amelia loved the university so much that she never left.

Gorgas Library.

The spiritual activity in Gorgas Library seems to focus on the area of the fourth floor. A number of students have claimed to hear things moving around on that floor at night, even when it had been closed for the day. Such noises are particularly interesting since it is impossible to access the fourth floor of the library after hours without a special key. On occasion, even the elevator opens on the fourth floor after it should be locked, despite the fact that no one is on board.

The curators of the Gorgas Library are certainly believers. Throughout the years since the library's construction, several of them have come to accept that they are not alone. A few have even claimed to have seen Amelia Gayle wandering through the stacks, making sure that her books are still in order. Those who have encountered Amelia are always clear that she does not invoke fear, at least no more than one might expect from a ghostly being. Instead, hers is a comforting presence, one that seems to care for the university and her students in death in the same way she did in life.

While Amelia seems the kindly ghost, there is another, more mysterious and more frightening specter that seems to walk among the stacks of

Gorgas Library. From whence it came and why it remains, no one knows, but many students have claimed to have witnessed an unidentified man, dressed completely in black, skulking around the halls of Gorgas. Some have reported that he even reaches out to them as they search for books, seeking to touch them or even grab their hands. Comforting this spirit certainly is not.

Even accounting for the mysterious figure in black, Gorgas Library is not thought of as a foreboding place. Rather, it is a home for the studious University of Alabama student or the one cramming at the last minute for a final exam. Amelia Gayle Gorgas watches over them all. To this day, she is still the University of Alabama's most motherly figure.

THE UNIVERSITY CLUB

Located on the corner of University Boulevard and Queen City Avenue is a house that fits every stereotype of what a southern antebellum home should be. The epitome of classical Greek Revival style, the home is a massive white-walled edifice with six equally massive white Ionic columns in the front. And you can't look at it without complete certainty that it is haunted.

Built in 1834 for the then astronomical sum of $14,000, the University Club was built on land originally reserved by the United States Congress for use by the University of Alabama. To finance the construction of the university, the land was sold to R.H. Walker. But it wasn't until the land passed to James H. Dearing, a steamboat tycoon and member of the Alabama legislature, that the house that would become the University Club was built.

Williams Nichols, the same renowned architect who designed the original University of Alabama campus, supervised the construction of the home. Two interesting architectural decisions mark the original design of the University Club. The first, a detached kitchen, was not particularly unusual for large homes at the time. Given their size and cost, owners couldn't risk that a fire in the kitchen—quite a common occurrence in that day and age—would threaten the main house. Firefighting services, those that even existed at the time, were primitive at best and wholly ineffective at worst. An attached kitchen was a disaster waiting to happen.

The magnificent structure's other interesting feature, on the other hand, was quite distinct. Built on the roof of the house was a central square platform from which the smoke of riverboats coming up the Black Warrior River with supplies from Mobile could be seen by the occupants. Given that Dearing made his fortune in the steamboat trade, no doubt he used this feature often.

The house's greatest fault turned out to be its proximity to campus. The students at the University of Alabama, known for their disorderly conduct and general rowdiness, would often find their way to the Dearing home in the middle of the night. The Dearings often woke in the morning to find their chickens missing and their carefully cultivated flowers trampled. Between the sounds of drunken singing and the acts of vandalism, the Dearings eventually gave up, selling the home in 1836.

Two years later, the house passed to the new governor of Alabama, Arthur Pendleton Bagby, as his official residence in Tuscaloosa, the state capital at the time. While the house came to be known as the Governor's Mansion, it only served in that capacity during Bagby's four-year term of office, from 1837 to 1841.

The home changed hands several more times before it passed to another of Alabama's notable names. In 1871, Henderson M. Somerville, a justice of the Alabama Supreme Court and the founder of the University of Alabama Law School, purchased the house. His family owned the home until the early 1900s. After that, the University Club passed from one family to another until, during the Second World War, it was designated the Tuscaloosa Service Center. In that role, it served as the entertainment center for soldiers passing through the city for the duration of the war.

In fact, the University Club filled its role as a social center so well that the university approached one of the city's leading families—the Warners—to assist it in acquiring the home for a lounge and social center for campus staff and faculty. After repairs and renovations, the home opened in 1946 under the name by which it is known today: the University Club.

To this day, the University Club remains the heart of the college's social life. The club often hosts official university functions, and it can also be reserved by members of the general public. The University Club has hosted hundreds of prospective students, honored graduates and wedding parties. As those souls have passed in and out the doors of the club, some have claimed to have encountered things within its walls that make them wonder if some of the previous inhabitants ever really left.

The University Club is one of those old-timey antebellum mansions that just screams southern gothic legends and ancient hauntings. According to the locals in Tuscaloosa, it has its share of both. The first thing one notices about the old Governor's Mansion is the feeling one gets upon entering the home.

It is a feeling that is difficult to describe but one that is fairly common in places that are purported to be haunted. Perhaps it is merely a trick of the mind, the result of the power of suggestion, but haunted locations simply feel *different*. It is a prickly feeling that rolls down your skin and the goose bumps that come with it. It is a dry mouth, a tightening of the throat, a feeling that every breath is somehow more difficult to take than it should be. And there's a silence, one of complete stillness, as if the living are afraid that by speaking or even breathing too loud, they will themselves wake the dead. Houses that are marked by paranormal activity are just a little bit off.

The University Club has this feeling and, if witnesses are to be believed, for good reason. There is a smell that seems as if it is always present within the halls of the University Club. Some say it is undefined, but the far more common claim is that it is the smell of flowers or perhaps old-fashioned floral perfume. People who experience this phenomenon often do so in the upper floors of the club, particularly on warm summer nights. On rare occasions, the smell is accompanied by a full-bodied apparition. Witnesses agree only

The University Club.

about the presence of the spirit; whether it is a man or a woman remains a mystery, though the accompanying smell indicates a female.

Whatever the case may be, one does not walk with ease through the University Club. There is a feeling that the eyes of some unseen watcher are always upon you. The lights come off and on, and there are noises that cannot be explained. We know of only one death, that of a female visitor to the club who apparently passed as a result of natural causes, in the long and storied history of the University Club. What haunts its halls is a mystery, whether a previous occupant or one who spent time at the club during his or her life. The only thing we can know for sure is that the party never ends at the University Club, not really.

WOODS QUAD

A stone's throw from the main quad and in the shadow of Amelia Gayle Gorgas Library sits Woods Quad. Woods Quad was, at one time, the heart of Alabama's campus. Woods Hall, for which the quad gets its name, was the first new building on campus following the destruction of the University of Alabama during the Civil War. Woods Hall is built in a style known as Gothic Revival, a style that, not surprisingly, echoed the great cathedrals and castles of medieval Europe.

Four stories tall, Woods Hall was initially called "the barracks," owing to the university's status as a military institution. Appropriately, it was patterned after buildings on the campus of the Virginia Military Institute. Woods Hall began as a dormitory, with a dining hall and classrooms on the first floor. In 1961, Woods Hall was given over to the Department of Art and Art History for its purposes.

The Department of Art has a long history at the University of Alabama. In 1945, Richard Zoellner brought to the university one of only two departments of fine art printmaking in the entire Southeast and the first art department in the state of Alabama. The university showed an early commitment to the arts, and it was one of the first art departments in the country accredited by the NASAD, the National Association of Schools of Art and Design. In addition to Woods Hall, Garland Hall, another neo-Gothic building, makes up the heart of the Department of Art.

Clark Hall, another of the neo-Gothic buildings that flank Woods Quad, was built in 1884. Clark Hall was meant to take on many of the functions

Woods Hall.

that Woods did not include, such as housing a library, meeting rooms and a chapel. Clark was, however, poorly constructed, and the building was unable to support its roof. Only an extensive renovation saved it from collapse.

In addition to Clark and Woods, Manly Hall is the final campus building on Woods Quad. Named after the university's second president, Basil Manly, the hall originally served as a dormitory before going on to house the Department of Religious Studies, as well as the university's campus literary magazine, the *Black Warrior Review*.

The ghost that haunts Woods Quad is one of the more romantic stories involving the University of Alabama campus. The spirit of William W. Alston is said to haunt the entire second story of Woods Hall. His ghost has been seen on more than one occasion by perplexed students who can't quite explain why a man in nineteenth-century clothing is wandering the upper veranda in the middle of the night. But William W. Alston does not haunt the halls of Woods Quad without good purpose. His is a story of honor, infamy and murder.

It was in the early months of 1877 when the lives and fates of Kibble J. Harrison and William W. Alston became forever tied. On a cold late winter morning, February 28, 1877, the two men walked to the opposite ends of the second-floor veranda of Woods Hall, the very same veranda that is said to be haunted to this day. Each man had a dueling pistol, and each man's purpose was to uphold his honor, even if it meant killing to do so. Both men turned. Both men fired. When the smoke cleared, one man lay dead, and the other was arrested for murder.

It had begun as a petty squabble between two of the newly planted fraternities on campus, Sigma Chi and Delta Kappa Epsilon. A dispute arose between the two groups, and what might have begun and ended with harsh words spoken and perhaps a few punches thrown quickly escalated into something far worse and far more dangerous. At some point, Alston publically questioned the integrity of Harrison's younger cousin, a harsh charge to be thrown at a young woman in that day and age. Under the code of southern gallantry in effect at the time, Harrison had only one choice. He challenged Alston to a duel.

Dueling had been illegal in Alabama since 1819, but Alston felt as though he had no choice but to accept. Any other action would have been a cowardly stain on his honor that could never be cleansed. (Apparently, a simple apology was out of the question.) On the morning of February 28, the two men, accompanied by their seconds, met at Woods Hall. They climbed to the second-floor veranda and stood in its center, back to back. Then they began the slow march to opposite ends, knowing that when they reached their destination, it would be time to fire. The two men turned, and shots rang out. Alston was struck, slumping over the veranda banister. He managed to fire off a shot, but it missed Harrison.

What happened next is shrouded in the fog of history. Whether the shot that struck Alston was fatal is up for dispute. But the fall from the second-story veranda to the hard ground below certainly was. Some say that Alston fell of his own accord after being hit by Harrison's shot. Others say that merely shooting Alston did not satisfy Harrison's need to defend the honor of his cousin. He wanted Alston dead, and so when he got the chance, he threw the injured Alston over the balcony, down to this death below.

Whatever the truth may be of what happened that day, when it was all over, Alston lay dead on the ground below. The local authorities were called to the scene, and Harrison was taken into custody. He was charged with murder, and the state had every intention of seeing him punished as severely as the law would allow. But first, he had to go before a jury of his peers. While the duel might have been outlawed several decades earlier, the notion of honor was far from dead.

Another view of Woods Hall.

There was, of course, no doubt that Harrison had killed Alston, and Harrison did not deny it. His argument for the defense of his cousin's honor, however, was quite convincing. When the jurors came back with their verdict, they were unanimous: not guilty. Harrison went home a free man. It is believed that the duel between Harrison and Alston may have been the last publicized duel in the South that ended in the death of one of the participants.

Whether because of his violent death, his sorrow over the initial wrong or the fact that his death was never avenged—either in the courts or otherwise—the students and faculty at the University of Alabama claim that Woods Quad is never empty. They say that Alston still walks the ground, particularly the second-floor veranda where he was shot. Students claim to feel bizarre cold spots on the second floor, even in the midst of hot summer days. Perhaps even stranger, visitors to Woods Hall have reported smelling the unmistakable odor of gunpowder in the corridors, and sometimes they even hear gunshots.

All we can know for sure about Woods Quad is that it is where the rebirth of the University of Alabama began. From that place rose, like a phoenix, a school that had burned in the fires of the Civil War. It was the sort of loss that could have been an irretrievable tragedy, and no doubt, even though the school has come far, the losses suffered in that bitter war were never truly undone. Today, the University of Alabama stands as a testament to people's dedication to rebuilding. It all began at Woods Hall, and if students and faculty are right, the history that Woods Hall has seen is not quite dead.

Sources and Interviews

A project like this would be impossible without the help of countless men and women who have passed down these stories throughout the generations. We spoke to many of them during our research. Some wanted to remain anonymous, while others were willing to go on the record. Their voices are here, within these pages. We thank them all, especially those mentioned below. A special thanks is due to the Tuscaloosa Historical Society and the Friends of Northport.

Books

Brackner, Joey, and Rae Hague Eighmey. *A Walk Through Greenwood Cemetery: An Historic Overview and Walking Tour*. Tuscaloosa, AL: Heritage Commission of Tuscaloosa County, 1992.

Clompton, Virginia Clay. *A Belle of the Fifties*. Tuscaloosa: University of Alabama Press, 1999.

Interviews

Donna Cox Baker, Susan Reynolds, February 23, 2012, Kilgore House.

Curtis Bonner, February 26, 2012, Greenwood Cemetery.

Ian Crawford, January 17, 2012, Old Tavern; January 31, 2012, Battle-
    Friedman House; February 2, 2012, Jemison Mansion.
Erin Harney, April 17, 2012, Gorgas House.
Emma Jean Melton, June 12, 2012, Murphy-Collins House.
Erika Rentschler, May 15, 2012, Smith Hall.

WEBSITES

Alabama Department of Archives and History, http://www.archives.
    state.al.us.
Alabama Women's Hall of Fame, http://www.awhf.org.
The Crimson and White, http://cw.ua.edu.
Encyclopedia.com, http://www.encyclopedia.com.
Encyclopedia of Alabama, http://www.encyclopediaofalabama.org/face/
    Home.jsp.
Rootsweb, http://www.rootsweb.ancestry.com.
Tuscaloosa County Preservation Society, http://historictuscaloosa.org.
Tuscaloosa News, http://www.tuscaloosanews.com.
Tuscaloosa Paranormal Research Group, http://tuscaloosaparanormal.com.
Wikipedia, http://www.wikipedia.org.